Competence in Ecclesiastical Tribunals

A Dissertation

Submitted to the Faculty of Sacred Sciences of
the Catholic University of America
in partial fulfilment of the requirements
for the Degree of

DOCTOR OF CANON LAW

BY THE

REV. THOMAS JOSEPH BURKE, S. T. B., J. C. L.
Of the Archdiocese of Philadelphia

1922

Nihil Obstat.

†THOMAS J. SHAHAN,

Censor Deputatus.

Washingtonii, D. C., die VIII Aprilis, 1922.

Imprimatur.

†MICHAEL J. CURLEY,

Archiepiscopus Baltimorensis.

Baltimorae, die VIII Aprilis, 1922.

TABLE OF CONTENTS

Table of Contents

INTRODUCTION: JUDICIARY POWER IN THE CHURCH.

The Church, as Christ's appointed Teacher, Ruler, and Sanctifier of mankind, has received from Him authority binding on the consciences of her subjects. As guardian and interpreter of the message of her divine Founder, she has the right to specify the meaning of the divine, as well as the ecclesiastical, law, in any particular case, and also to judge whether a given act is in harmony or at variance with that law. This power is known as the judiciary power, and may be defined to be the right of declaring or proposing in an obligatory manner what actions of its subjects are conformable to the law and what actions are not conformable, and the legitimate effects of that conformity or non-conformity.

This power, exercised from the time of the foundation of the Church, flows logically from its constitution. Established by Christ as a perfect society, independent of the civil society in things relating to the spiritual order, by reason of its end and the means necessary to realize that end, the Church ought to possess in itself all the attributes, rights and privileges enjoyed by a perfect society. The Synagogue, which was but a figure of the Church to come, made laws, judged transgressors, and imposed sentence on the children of Israel. It therefore appears altogether conformable to the teaching of Christ and of reason that equal power should be conferred on the Church by Him who came to give men striking testimony of His divine mission, and of the power, absolute in its order, which He possessed.

Devoid of the power to govern, no society can really exist and attain its end. A multitude of wills seeking to attain the same end necessarily requires common and efficacious guidance. Hence, when it pleased our Saviour to form into a perfect society all those who believed in Him, He could not but endow this society with the authority requisite for the accomplishment of its mission. In other words, when He established heads and rulers invested with legislative power, He likewise conferred on them judiciary and coercive powers, for a law supposes the right to judge the guilty and to inflict punishment.

Since there are many who have judicial power in the external forum, it may be of some assistance to enumerate those so endowed, together with pertinent Canons of the New Code. Such a division will have no reference to their diversity by reason of the object they can judge, the persons subjected to their judicial power, or the grades or instances in which they can judge.

They are: (1) The Sovereign Pontiff in person (Cc. 218-220, 1556); (2) the Sacred Congregation of the Holy Office (C. 247); (3) the Sacred Congregation of Rites (C. 253, para. 3); (4) the Apostolic Signatura (Cc. 1602-1605); the Sacred Roman Rota (Cc. 1598-1601); (6) Metropolitans as such (Cc. 1594-1596); (7) Diocesan Archbishops and Bishops (C. 1572, sqq.); (8) Vicars Apostolic (C. 294); (9) Prefects Apostolic (C. 294); (10) permanent Apostolic Administrators (C. 315); (11) Pro-Vicars Apostolic, when there is no Vicar Apostolic or when he has no jurisdiction (C. 309, para. 2); (12) Pro-Prefects Apostolic in the same circumstances (C. 309, para. 2); (13) Abbots or Prelates *nullius* (C. 323); (14) Officials of Bishops, even though they have the same power as the Bishop (C. 1573); (15) Vicars Capitular and Administrators (Cc. 431, para. 1, 432, para. 1); (16) Supreme Moderators of exempt religious (C. 501); (17) Supreme Superiors of Monastic Congregations, in cases of appeal from the local Abbot (C. 1594, para. 4), in controversies between two monasteries, if so permitted by their Constitutions (C. 1579, para. 2), or if special decrees of the Holy See permit it (C. 501, para. 3); (18) local Abbots, if the monastery be *sui juris* (C. 1579, para. 1); (19) Provincial Superiors of exempt religious, if no other provisions are made in Constitutions (C. 1579, para. 2); (20) other Superiors of the same religious, if so provided for in their Constitutions (arguing from the words *nisi aliud in constitutionibus caveatur* of the same Canon); (21) General and Provincial Chapters of exempt religious in accordance with their Constitutions (C. 501); (22) Supreme Councils of exempt religious or of Monastic Congregations in causes for the dismissal of religious (C. 665); (23) Legates of the Holy See, in settling controversies as to competence arising between tribunals having no higher court in the country (C. 1612, para. 2); (24) all to whom the above mentioned judges, except those enumerated in n. 22, shall have legitimately delegated judicial power (C. 199), and their delegated power is to be regulated in accordance with Canons 1606, 1607.[1]

This hierarchy of judiciary power is the work of ecclesiastical law only, for in the Apostolic College there was no other supremacy established than that of Peter, and we find no share of it attributed to one apostle more than to another. During the course of ages, the extension of the Church on the one hand, and on the other, the difficulty of maintaining immediate and continual communication between the Sovereign Pontiff and the Bishops, between the Bishops and the ever increasing number of the faithful, caused the Church, little by little, to imitate in its external jurisdiction the organization of the provinces of the empire.

---

[1] Noval, *De Processibus*, pp. 32, 33.

I. JURISDICTION AND COMPETENCE.

1. General Notion of Forum and Competence.

The word *forum* is a juridicial term frequently employed in ecclesiastical law. We speak, for instance, of the internal and external fora, of the penitential forum, of the secular forum, and of the ecclesiastical forum. Whence does the word come; and what is its precise meaning? Etymologically, the word *forum* designates the public place in which justice is administered and sentence is pronounced in cases brought up for trial. In a metaphorical sense, it is often used to denote justice itself, or the tribunal which passes judgment, the place in which jurisdiction is exercised, and jurisdiction itself; hence the frequent occurrence of such expressions as the forum of conscience, the ecclesiastical or secular forum, the contentious forum—which is called *criminal,* when it deals with the prosecution of crime, and *civil,* when it deals with the possession of rights or property—and the competent forum.

By the term *competent forum* we mean the tribunal of the judge to whose jurisdiction the defendant (*reus*) is subject, and to which tribunal the defendant should, or at least can be, brought by the plaintiff (*actor*). It thus designates and implies both the jurisdiction which is exercised in settling controversies, and the place or tribunal in which the controversies are settled; so much so that the union of the two elements constitutes its definition.

An *incompetent forum* is a tribunal lacking judicial power, either in the cause or against the defendant, and before which tribunal the defendant cannot or should not be brought.

The competent forum is divided into *legal* or *constitutional,* which is constituted by law and determined for the cause for which it is held; and *conventional* or *prorogued,* which is constituted by law inasmuch as the institution of tribunals and the communication of judicial power is the work of legitimate legal authority, but it is determined by the will of the parties (cf. C. 1565, para. 2). The *common* or *general* competent forum is that which is constituted for all persons and causes, e. g., the diocesan and metropolitan tribunals, the Rota and the Signatura; the *singular* or *special* competent forum is that which is constituted for certain persons, e. g., exempt religious, or for some causes, e. g., the tribunal of the Holy Office for causes concerning the Faith.

A forum is called *universal,* if its power extends to the universal Church; otherwise it is called *particular.* It is called *ordinary,* when persons or things are subjected to it by general rule; *extraordinary,* if they are subjected to it by exception, e. g., for exempt religious, the diocesan court in those things by which they are subject to the Ordinary. The name *necessary* is given to a tribunal when by a ruling of the law it alone should be approached (C. 1560). This does not bind under pain of nullity. That is called free or *voluntary* which may be selected from many, e. g., those mentioned in Cc. 1561-1566. Another division is made into those *absolutely* and *relatively* competent. The *supreme* forum is that of the Holy See; others are *inferior.*

Exclusive of any consideration of the grades or instances of trials, there are in general sixteen methods or titles by which a forum is selected. Of these, the first four have *absolute* competence; the others, *relative* competence. They are: (1) Apostolic Primatial forum, because of the immediate subjection of all the faithful to the Roman Pontiff by reason of his primacy (Cc. 1569; 1557, para. 3); (2) Apostolic forum, by reason of the immediate subjection of special persons to the Roman Pontiff, on account of the concessions made in the New Code (C. 1557, para. 1); (3) forum of Faith, by reason of subjection to the tribunal of the Holy Office (C. 247);

(4) Rotal forum, by reason of subjection to the ordinary Tribunals of the Holy See (C. 1557, para. 2); (5) necessary forum (C. 1560); (6) forum of domicile or quasi-domicile (C. 1561); (7) forum when traveling in Rome (C. 1562, para. 1); (8) forum when sojourning for a year in Rome (C. 1562, para. 2); (9) forum of religious (C. 1563); (10) forum of *vagi* (C. 1563); (11) forum by reason of the location of the object (C. 1564); (12) forum by reason of contract (C. 1565, para. 1); (13) forum by contracting parties (C. 1565, para. 2); (14) forum by reason of the commission of crime (C. 1566); (15) forum of connected causes (C. 1567); (16) forum by reason of preoccupancy (C. 1568).

2. General Notion of Competence and Jurisdiction.

Competence, in general, implies jurisdiction, for that judge is called competent who has the power of applying the law to certain persons in certain causes. Competence properly so called is jurisdiction over persons and their causes; not over persons alone, nor over only one cause. It very often happens that a judge has jurisdiction over certain persons, but only over one species of causes, not over all causes that can arise among them. This is verified, for example in a Bishop. He exercises jurisdiction over the members of his diocese, but only in ecclesiastical causes. Likewise a judge may have jurisdiction over a certain kind of causes, provided those causes arise between certain persons and not between others. Bishops have the power of judging and inflicting punishment on delinquent clerics, but only those of their own diocese.

Although the persons may be numbered among those over whom the judge exercises jurisdiction, if the cause between them is not likewise subjected to his jurisdiction, that judge lacks the power of judging. Moreover, though the cause may be within the jurisdiction of the judge, unless the same jurisdiction is extended to the persons to be judged in that cause, judicial power is lacking.

Competence is the jurisdiction by which a judge can begin a trial about some charge that has been advanced. But not every judge can put an end to a controversy, because all judges cannot indiscriminately put an end to all contentions. Hence competence and jurisdiction differ, although this difference is not always strictly observed. Competence not only differs from jurisdiction as a species from its genus, but also as the concrete from the abstract. Jurisdiction signifies the power of ruling the faithful in all things necessary for obtaining the end of the Church; competence signifies the determined power of judging attributed to a certain judge with respect to certain causes and in a certain territory. It is important that we thus distinguish competence from jurisdiction, because we are thereby confronted with the logical question: what are the reasons for limiting the power of jurisdiction, and thus determining competence?

The reasons why the positive law assigns limits to the power of jurisdiction of judges, determining their competency, may be sought for, partly in the fundamental principles of public law, and partly in private utility. The reasons flowing from the former so affect competency as to render it *necessary* and *absolute,* and cannot be otherwise employed in trials, at the pleasure of contending parties, as for example, the competence of an ecclesiastical judge in ecclesiastical causes. On the other hand those qualifications of competence introduced chiefly on account of the good of individuals, are for a time subject to their choice and disposition, or they may be changed for a while, as for example, by prorogation, that is, by extending the competency of the judge. Hence this competency may be called *relative,* as distinguished from the necessary competency arising from the public law.

Because jurisdiction, or competence, of a tribunal is the foundation of every judicial trial, so much so that the lack of it may subject the trial to nullity, we can readily understand how important it is for the judge, before everything else, to find out whether he is competent. Not every judge can settle all causes, but only those causes which are subjected to his jurisdiction. Hence, canonists, after treating of competence in general, determine (1) what causes pertain to the ecclesiastical judge in common with the civil judge; and (2) those causes in which the ecclesiastical judge is either doubtfully competent or incompetent.

3. Causes of Mixed Tribunals (*Mixti Fori*).

Those causes are called *mixti fori,* or of mixed tribunals, in which both the Church and the civil power are equally competent.[2] They cannot be absolutely referred to either power, for each is capable of taking cognizance of them. This capability of taking cognizance is derived primarily from the nature of mixed causes themselves, and in other causes it may be conferred by privilege, or by the express or tacit concession of either power, or by immemorial custom, which has come to regard such causes as falling within the competence of both powers. These causes admit of preoccupancy (*praeventionis*), so that that power judges which first undertakes the case, thereby excluding the other power from judging.

In general all those causes and only those causes are *mixti fori* which (1) deal with something of itself temporal but having a separable spiritual element, or some special reference to the spiritual, equally separable from the temporal aspect; and (2) are restricted to a temporal element or aspect. In these circumstances the civil power is competent, because by the civil law, attributing to it the power to provide for the temporal prosperity of the citizens, it can pass judgment on every temporal matter not inseparably connected with a spiritual thing or with the supernatural order. But the Church, since it is competent in the principal or spiritual

---

[2] Can. 1553, para. 2.

element is also necessarily competent in the accessory or temporal element. For it is eminently fitting that the accessory should follow the nature of its principal, when there is no repugnance, and there is certainly no repugnance for the Church to have and to exercise judiciary power in temporal matters. With St. Paul we may say, "Know you not that we shall judge angels? How much more things of this world?"[3]

In causes *mixti fori,* as in all other causes, some are civil or contentious, others are criminal. In particular the following civil causes are *mixti fori*:

(1) Those concerning the value of an act or a contract entered into by lay persons originally belonged to the secular power. But if the act or contract has been confirmed by an oath, because of the spiritual quality of an oath, its execution may be demanded by either power. Any investigation into the value of the oath will pertain solely to the ecclesiastical judge.

(2) Concerning the restoration of the dowry after a legal separation, exclusive of any investigation into the separation itself.

(3) Concerning the revenues of benefices, exclusive of all examination as to the benefice or the right of receiving revenues from it.

(4) Concerning the succession of children in certain rights of the nobility, without investigating their legitimacy.

(5) Concerning a spiritual fact alone; e. g., whether a person was baptized, provided (a) the investigation does not involve a question as to the validity of the act, and the case is handled because of the consequent temporal effects, e. g., the right of inheritance;[4] but not if there are spiritual effects, e. g., the capacity of receiving sacred orders; (b) it is not concerned with the possession of some spiritual rights, e. g., *jus patronatus.*

---

[3] I Cor. VI. 3.

[4] Conc. Trid., Sess. XXII, cap. 8, *de. ref.*

(6) Causes of deserving persons (*miserabilium personarum*). They are called *miserabiles personae* who are worthy of special consideration, such as widows, orphans, the poor, the oppressed, captives, and the like. Especially in cases of forcible oppression, deprivation of property, or negligence on the part of the civil judge in administering justice, should the ecclesiastical judge take cognizance.

(7) Cases concerning the merely civil effects of marriage belong to the civil magistrate,[5] if such effects constitute the principal action in the case; but if they are incidental or accessory questions they can be examined and decided also by the ecclesiastical judge.[6]

Those criminal causes are called *mixti fori* which are concerned with crimes prohibited and punished by canon and civil laws. They include homicide, sodomy, perjury, blasphemy, divination, magic, theft of ecclesiastical property, and certain crimes against marriage, e. g., adultery, abortion and bigamy.

Ordinaries, as a rule, should not proceed against crimes which may be prosecuted in the civil or in the ecclesiastical court, if the accused is a layman and if the civil authority is already prosecuting him, thereby safeguarding the public welfare.[7] One of the principal reasons for punishing crime is the restoration of public order. The Church has been appointed by her divine Founder as the custodian of public morality. She is therefore entitled to prosecute criminal offences against morality if the civil authority neglects to do so. Hence the ecclesiastical authority cannot lawfully be rejected as prosecutor by the lay criminal court, if the public welfare is involved and the civil law provides no punishment for such crimes.

An offence which violates a law of the Church only is by its very nature punishable by ecclesiastical authority alone, but the Church may at times, if it

---

[5] Can. 1016.

[6] Can. 1961.

[7] Can. 1933, para. 3.

judges such help necessary or opportune, requisition the assistance of the civil power. An offence which violates a law of the civil authority only is subject to punishment by the civil authority in its own right, save for the exceptions made when clerics are to be summoned by a civil or lay court.[8] Moreover, as civil offences are sometimes also moral disorders and sins, the Church is competent to judge them, because of the sin,[9] and to inflict punishment upon them.[10] Offences which violate the law of both Church and State may be punished by both authorities.[11]

If a doubt should arise over competence in causes *mixti fori* the matter is to be settled in a friendly manner, otherwise the Church should decide the controversy.

In causes *mixti fori,* as has previously been said, preoccupancy (*praeventio*) is permitted.[12] By reason of preoccupancy (*ratione praeventionis*), when two or more judges are equally competent, that judge has the right to try the case who first legitimately proceeds against the defendant by a citation.[13]

Should a plaintiff venture to bring suit before a secular court in a matter that has already been brought before an ecclesiastical court, he may be punished by the lawful ecclesiastical superior, if scandal was given or the importance of the case requires a punishment; and that punishment may be meted out without previous warning or threat.[14] He is likewise deprived of his right to plead before the ecclesiastical tribunal his cause against the same person in that same matter and in those matters connected with the matter at issue.[15] The punishment depends on the giving of scandal or the

[8] Cans. 120, 614, 680, 1553, para. 1, n. 3.

[9] Competence "because of the sin" is an allusion to the famous decretal *Novit* of Innocent III, cf. Nussi, *Conventiones*, pp. 92, 105, 151, 185, 312.

[10] Cans. 1553, para. 1, n. 2; 2198.

[11] Can. 2198.

[12] Cans. 1553, para. 2; 2198.

[13] Cans. 1568, 1711-1725.

[14] Cans. 1554, 2222.

[15] Can. 1554.

special gravity of the offense; but the deprivation of rights in that cause is *ipso facto,* even though no scandal was given, and without distinction as to the gravity of the transgression. Formerly, excommunication was decreed for those who refused to accept the ecclesiastical tribunal in mixed matters, and other punishments were inflicted on ecclesiastics who attempted a change of tribunals.[16]

4. Doubtful Competence.

A doubt concerning competence may arise between two judges, as to which of them is entitled to hear the case. This doubt should be settled by the immediate Superior or the next higher court, according to the rules of appeal. If the judges belong to different higher courts, the proper tribunal to settle the dispute is the higher court of the one to which the case was first brought. If they have no higher court, the question is settled by the Apostolic Delegate or by the Apostolic Signatura.[17]

Doubtful competence arising between the Sacred Congregations, Tribunals or Offices of the Roman Curia is settled by an assembly of Cardinals specially designated by the Roman Pontiff for each individual case.[18]

It may also happen that a question of competent forum arise between an ecclesiastical judge and a civil judge. In such an event the definitive sentence is to be given by the ecclesiastical judge, because he is of a higher order.[19]

Canon Law also considers valid the acts of a putative judge. A judge can be putative because his jurisdiction is null, e. g., that conferred by a simoniacal bishop, or because his jurisdiction was conferred for a certain

---

[16] Martin V, Const. *Ad reprimendas insolentias,* Feb. 1, 1428.

[17] Can. 1612, explained more fully under "Competence of the Apostolic Signatura," para. 3, n. (f).

[18] Can. 245.

[19] Lega, *De Judiciis Ecclesiasticis,* Pars. I, para. 351.

length of time already elapsed, or because his jurisdiction has been revoked.

In case of common error the lack of jurisdiction in a putative judge is likewise supplied, for the common law is intended for the common welfare, and an error on the part of a few should not affect the populace generally.[20]

Hence provision is made for the common good and the public security as well as for the tranquillity of conscience by reaffirming[21] the well-known principle that the Church supplies the necessary jurisdiction when a common error or a positive doubt arises. The same effect is produced by a probable doubt, i. e., in this case one which for certain reasons inclines more to the side of the power being vested in the person whose court is sought. The common error, to obtain this effect, must be accompanied by a *titulus coloratus*, or a colored title to the office one exercises. An intruder, one who assumes the office of judge without the authority of a Superior having power to confer it, has no claim to the validation of his acts.[22]

5. Incompetence.

One of the chief duties of a judge, before he cites or admits anyone to his court for trial, is to see whether or not he is competent either by reason of his jurisdiction over the person, or by reason of the matter he is to judge.[23] How to discern and determine the competent judge in any cause is a question of great moment, for an error therein may expose the sentence to the danger of nullity.

With the exception of the Roman Pontiff, who is the supreme judge in the Church, judges do not enjoy the plenitude of judicial power. Some of them can judge

[20] Lega, *loc. cit.;* Bouix, *De Judiciis Ecclesiasticis,* I, pp. 131-135.
[21] Can. 209.
[22] Reiffenstuel, *Jus Canonicum,* Tom. II, Tit. I, n. 200.
[23] Can. 1609, para. 1.

only certain kinds of causes or persons, others can judge only in certain places. In reference to these causes, persons or places, they are competent judges; in reference to others, they are incompetent. Hence the obligation incumbent on every judge before a trial to consider the various reasons which constitute a competent forum. Moreover, if he is a delegated judge, he must be aware of the tenor of the rescript under which he officiates, lest he exceed the limits of his power.[24]

Since competence is limited jurisdiction, incompetence may be defined to be the lack of judicial power in a judge with respect to the controversy submitted to his decision. There is a twofold distinction made in incompetence—relative and absolute. *Relative incompetence* flows from the law defending private rights, and is that by which a judge is incompetent in relation to this time, or place, or cause. A sentence passed by a relatively incompetent judge is valid, though illicit. *Absolute incompetence* has its source in the principles of public right, and is that which can in no manner be made good. A sentence passed by an absolutely incompetent judge is null. It is of great importance, therefore, to know when incompetence is absolute, inasmuch as it then renders a sentence irreparably null.[25]

Absolute incompetence is sought for under four heads: (1) by reason of the person to be judged;[26] (2) by reason of the object of the trial;[27] (3) by reason of the degree or instance of a trial;[28] (4) by reason of the avocation of a cause to the Holy See.[29]

No one can be called as a defendant for trial in the first instance except before an ecclesiastical judge whose competence is determined by one of the titles in

[24] Delegated jurisdiction is regulated by Cans. 196-210.
[25] Can. 1892, n. 1.
[26] Cans. 1556, 1557, paras. 1, 2; 1558.
[27] Cans. 247, 254, 655, 1576, para. 1; 1603.
[28] Cans. 1571, 1572, 1579, 1599, 1612.
[29] Cans. 1557, para. 3; 1558.

Canons 1560-1568. A judge who is supported by none of these titles is said to be *relatively* incompetent.[30]

The defendant, when summoned, must appear before the judge. If he doubts the competence of the judge, he may, after hearing the cause of the summons, enter a plea (*exceptio*) against the competence of the judge. Such a plea is for the defence of the accused and is called *declinatoria fori*. It does not destroy the right of the plaintiff to take action, but only suspends for a time the progress of the trial, because it is thought the judge is incompetent. This plea must be made before the case is contested (*ante contestationem litis*), unless the reason for the plea first occurred after the trial had been begun, e. g., if the judge then became related to the other litigant by affinity in the direct line; or unless the party making the plea affirmed with an oath that he had no previous knowledge of the incompetence of the judge.[31] However, exception may be taken to the competency of the judge in any phase or stage of the trial, provided the alleged incompetency is absolute.[32]

Neglect on the part of the defendant to propose a plea against the competence of the judge must not be supplied by any aid from the judge.[33] This is a reasonable prohibition, since a judge should apply the law in accordance with the information secured in the course of the trial.[34] Furthermore, to volunteer such advice savors of partiality, intolerable in a judge, who must be above suspicion. If, however, the case concerns the public welfare or the salvation of souls the judge may and ought, if possible, to supply deficient proofs and use privately acquired knowledge to insure a fair trial.[35]

A judge accused of incompetence sees to that accusation himself.[36] No distinction is made by the Code

[30] Can. 1559, paras. 1, 2.
[31] Can. 1628, para. 1.
[32] Can. 1628, para. 2.
[33] Can. 1619, para. 1.
[34] Can. 1869.
[35] Cans. 1619, para. 2; 1759, para. 3; 1975, para. 1.
[36] Can. 1610, para. 1.

as to whether the judge has ordinary or delegated jurisdiction, or whether he constitutes a tribunal or is a member of a collegiate tribunal.

A plea of *relative* incompetence may be advanced because of the lack of one of the reasons stated in Canons 1560-1568 for the establishment of a competent forum. In the event of a plea of *relative* incompetence, if the judge declares himself competent, his decision admits of no appeal.[37] In regard to a plea of *absolute* incompetence, although the Code is silent, we may deduce from a contrary argument that his decision does admit of appeal.

A judge perceiving in any state of the trial that he is absolutely incompetent is bound to make a declaration to that effect.[38] By the phrase, "in any state of the trial," is meant (1) the period preceding the contesting of the case (*ante litis contestationem*), i. e., while the judge is examining the charge (*libellus*) and the response of the defendant to the citation; (2) while he is sitting in judgment, i. e., from the contesting of the case up to pronouncing sentence in the first trial; (3) even after he has given an interlocutory sentence; (4) before or during the trial of second instance, if the complaint of nullity of the sentence of the first judge is proposed either by way of a perpetual exception or by way of an action.[39]

This declaration of *absolute* incompetence the judge is bound to make in virtue of his office, apart from any plea proposed by the litigants, for he is obliged under penalty of reparation to avoid invalid acts.[40]

If the judge declares himself incompetent, the party who thinks himself inconvenienced—the plaintiff, should the plea have been proposed by the defendant—may appeal within a space of ten days to the immediately

[37] Can. 1610, para. 2.
[38] Can. 1611.
[39] Can. 1893.
[40] Can. 1625, paras. 1, 2.

higher tribunal.[41] This regulation is applicable whether the declaration is made at the request of one of the parties or *ex officio* by the judge, or whether it concerns absolute or relative incompetence.

II. COMPETENT FORUM OR TRIBUNAL.

1. General Rule for Determining Competent Forum.

In ecclesiastical as well as in civil courts, when judicial proceedings are about to be instituted against any person, it is of prime importance to ascertain which is the *forum competens,* or that particular tribunal which has competence in the case.

How do we know which ecclesiastical judge has competence in this or that ecclesiastical cause? It will be noted that the definition of competent forum is worded with respect to the defendant, because, as a general rule, the plaintiff should follow the forum to which the defendant in a cause is subject. Hence, even when the plaintiff belongs to a different forum from the defendant, he must institute proceedings before the latter's forum. All this follows from the legal maxim: *actor sequitur forum rei.* If the defendant is subject to several forums, e. g., in one place by reason of domicile, in another place by reason of a contract made there, the choice is left to the plaintiff.[42]

In every trial there is one who complains and one who is complained against, one who accuses and one who is accused. The one is called the *actor* or plaintiff; the other, the *reus* or defendant.

The *actor* or plaintiff receives his name from the act by which he seeks something which the law admits

---

[41] Can. 1610, para. 3.
[42] Can. 1559, para. 3.

he has the right to seek, and in Canon Law he is variously designated as *actor, agere in judicio, habere personam standi in judicio.*

Strictly speaking, the *actor* is the litigant who first proposes an action or petition by imploring the services of a judge, or by beginning a trial. In a wider sense, any of the litigants may be called an *actor,* so long as he seeks or proposes something in a trial. Hence, if a defendant does not deny the charge alleged in the petition of the plaintiff, but asks that another fact be admitted modifying or qualifying the charge of the plaintiff, he becomes an *actor* in that petition—*reus excipiendo fit actor.*

The *actor* may be a physical person, a moral non-collegiate person, e. g., a church, seminary, etc., or a moral collegiate person, e. g., a cathedral chapter, or a religious order,[40] since moral persons are capable of rights and therefore of actions to protect those rights.

In the same trial there can be one or more *actores* or plaintiffs against one or more *rei* or defendants. Generally, the *actor* voluntarily institutes proceedings, but sometimes he is obliged to do so, e. g., the rector of a church, the administrator of a pious undertaking, a guardian or procurator, if the rights or property they are bound to protect have suffered injury.

The *reus* or defendant is the person summoned for trial by the judge, and from whom some reparation is sought by the plaintiff. The *reus,* or defendant, is so called, not precisely from *reitas,* or his being charged with crime, but rather from *respondere,* or from his obligation to answer to the summons of the judge who has him brought to trial, whence he is also called *reus conventus,* or simply *conventus.* A defendant can be a physical person, or a moral collegiate person, and in contentious, but not in criminal, causes a moral non-collegiate person. Ordinarily, a defendant becomes such by necessity, but he can sometimes become one voluntarily,

---

[40] Cf. Cans. 99-105.

when, for example, in the citation there is contained the phrase *ut si qui sint,* or *qui se velint opponere, compareant.*

What persons are disqualified from acting as plaintiffs or defendants? As in civil so in ecclesiastical courts, not all may appear as plaintiffs or defendants, some being incapacitated by the natural law, others by the ecclesiastical law, others by both laws. Ecclesiastical law recognizes all human beings as persons, capable of rights, but requires for the exercise of rights certain necessary qualities of intellect and will.

First the general rule is laid down that any one not prevented by Canon Law may act as plaintiff; but any person legitimately cited by a competent judge must appear for trial,[44] otherwise criminals might derive much profit from their malice.

Those who are under a sentence, either declaratory or condemnatory, of excommunication, either as *vitandi*[45] or *tolerati,*[46] are allowed to appear as plaintiffs in ecclesiastical trials only in case they wish to plead against the legitimacy or justice of the sentence of excommunication. But if they wish to avoid spiritual injury or damage they must act by proxy. In all other causes they are to be prohibited from acting as plaintiffs. All other persons, though excommunicated, may act as plaintiffs; but all excommunicated persons, even *vitandi,* if called into court in some other case, must obey.[47]

To act personally in trials requires a normally developed mind and will. Since infants, minors, and those adults who lack either the actual or habitual use of reason cannot properly exercise personal rights, ecclesiastical law obliges their parents or guardians to

[44] Can. 1646.
[45] Cans. 2343, para. 1, n. 1; 2258, 2232, para. 1, 2223, para. 4, 2225.
[46] Cans. 2223, para. 4; 2232, para. 1.
[47] Cans. 1654, 2263.

act as plaintiffs or defendants in their stead.[48] However, it may happen that parents or guardians have personal interests of their own involved in the trial, and that these interests conflict with those of the children or wards. In that case the children or wards are to act through a guardian appointed by the judge.[49]

In spiritual matters, and matters closely connected with them, minors who have attained the use of reason[50] may act as plaintiffs or defendants without the consent of their parents or guardians; and after the completion of their fourteenth year the minors themselves may act without a procurator. Before they have completed their fourteenth year, *impuberes* must be represented at trials by a guardian appointed by the Ordinary, or by a procurator whom they have chosen with the approval of the Ordinary.[51]

Religious may not act as plaintiffs without the consent of their Superiors. There are only three exceptions to this general rule:

(1) When a religious wishes to prosecute against the institute to which he belongs rights acquired by reason of his religious profession, he may proceed without the Superior's permission.

(2) If a religious lawfully dwells outside the enclosure and is compelled to defend his rights, he may do so without the Superior's permission.

(3) Individual religious may denounce their own Superior without that Superior's consent.[52]

---

[49] Can. 1648, para. 2.
[50] Presumed after the completion of the seventh year (Can. 88, para. 3).
[51] Can. 1648, para. 3.
[52] Can. 1648, nn. 1, 2, 3.
[48] Can. 1648, para. 1.

2. Forum by Reason of the Connection or Bearing of Causes.

An ecclesiastical judge also obtains competence by reason of the connection (*connexio*) or bearing (*continentia*) which one cause has with or upon another, so that such causes are to be tried by one and the same judge, unless the law expressly forbids it.[53]

Those causes are said to be *connected* which are in a manner linked together, but which can be separately examined and defined; they have a *bearing* on each other when the decision of one cause is required before that of the other can be given. The difference is so slight that both terms may be considered as having a synonymous import. Hence a judge can take cognizance of and decide all questions or matters which in the course of the trial come up incidentally to, or in connection with, the main cause or issue at hand. This holds good for delegated as well as ordinary judges, for the Canon makes no distinction. Judges not only *can,* but *ought to,* take cognizance of such causes. This was the wording and interpretation of the old law,[54] and those Canons which restate the old law without change must be interpreted upon the authority of the old law, and therefore in the light of the teaching of approved authors.[55]

What causes are said to be connected or have a bearing on each other? Positive law has not stated specifically which causes are to be thus designated, hence it remains for the judge to decide. Connection or bearing is usually sought for in three things: (1) in the persons assembled for trial, e. g., in the trial of the perpetrator and the instigator of a crime; (2) in the action or controverted right, e. g., between the principal question of the division of an estate and the incidental

[53] Can. 1567.
[54] Reiffenstuel, *loc. cit.,* n. 145.
[55] Can. 6, n. 2.

question of the legitimacy of the offspring; (3) in the title or fact upon which the trial is begun, e. g., in a trial against a debtor, and that which may be brought against his bondsman. Moreover, when one or two of these three reasons are common to two causes the causes are said to be connected or have a bearing on each other.

As a general rule, the judge who sees to one cause should also judge the connected cause, unless there is a positive law against it. This objection occurs in all causes with respect to which the law designates some judge: (1) *absolutely competent,* e. g., the Pope alone may judge Cardinals;[56] (2) *exclusively competent,* namely, in those causes which have a necessary forum;[57] (3) *prohibited from judging,* e. g., because of blood relationship or affinity with one of the contending parties;[58] (4) *obliged to exclude,* either *ex officio* or at the request of one of the parties, a litigant under a condemnatory or declaratory sentence of excommunication;[59] (5) presented with the power of *judging only one aspect* of the case, e. g., in criminal damage suits, if the difficulty of an equitable settlement proves too great, the Ordinary may refer the solution of this matter to the civil court.[60]

The New Code, therefore, confirms the principle of the old law, *continentiam causarum non esse dividendam,* because naturally connected causes are more expeditiously handled by the one judge, there is less danger of conflicting sentences, and an unnecessary expenditure of time and money is thereby avoided.

---

[56] Cans. 1557, para. 1, n. 2; 1558.
[57] Can. 1560.
[58] Can. 1613.
[59] Can. 1628; para. 3.
[60] Can. 1951, para. 3.

3. Forum by Reason of Preoccupancy (*Praeventionis*).

The concurrence of forums consists in this, that two or more tribunals are with respect to one and the same cause equally competent before the inception of the cause. The forums which may sometimes concur are those by reason of domicile, by reason of the location of the object, by reason of contract, by reason of the connection of causes. The domiciliary forum is a proper and natural forum, that where the object is located or where a contract is made in less proper and quasi-accidental. Hence it follows that if the forum of domicile concurs with either of the other two, the judge in the place of domicile, if he summons the defendants on account of a contract made elsewhere, impedes the competence of the judge in the place of contract. Should the judge in the place of contract first issue the summons he thereby impedes the competence of the judge by reason of domicile.

Some authors[61] are of the opinion that the forum of domicile does not concur with the forum in the place where the object is located, but that the latter prevails. Sometimes a trial can be begun only in the forum where the object is located, e. g., when it is a case of restitution of plunder, etc., by accident then the domiciliary forum does not concur with that in which the object is located.

Canon 1568 thus legislates on the concurrence of tribunals: by reason of preoccupancy (*praeventionis*), when two or more judges are equally competent, that judge has the right to try the case, who first legitimately proceeds against the defendant by a citation. Preoccupancy is the act by which one of several equally competent judges anticipates by a legitimate citation the other judges in beginning a case. The judges must be *equally* competent. Should one of them be the judge of

[61] Cf. Schmalzgrueber, *Jus Ecclesiasticum*, Tom. II, Pars. I, Tit. II, nn. 56-58.

the *necessary* forum,[62] that forum must be approached under grave obligation, but not under pain of nullity, for the incompetence of other judges in causes pertaining to a necessary forum is relative.[63]

If one of the judges is competent, e. g., by reason of the location of the object in an action to recover possession of something, and another is competent by reason of domicile, they are not equally competent; the competence of the former is necessary, while that of the latter is voluntary. Hence preoccupancy could not take place, but if the judge of the domicile tried the case, his decision, though illicit, would be valid.

The citation, or the act by which the defendant is first called to court by the mandate of the judge to undergo trial, in all these cases must be legitimately executed. Hence, the intimation must be a written command of the judge to the defendant. It must state clearly the name of the judge, the nature of the complaint at least in general terms, the name and surname of the plaintiff and defendant, the place where and the time when the defendant must appear. The summons must be sealed with the seal of the court, and signed by the judge or his auditor and the notary.[64] These elements are so essential to a summons that the omission of one subjects the entire proceedings to nullity.[65]

When the defendant has been informed,[66] the cause is said to have been begun; the judge or court before whom the action was brought becomes competent, and preoccupancy may no longer take place.[67]

---

[62] Can. 1560, enumerates the causes that have a necessary forum.

[63] Can. 1559, para. 2.

[64] Can. 1715, paras. 1, 2.

[65] Can. 1723.

[66] The intimation or conveyance of the summons is made in accordance with Cans. 1717-1722.

[67] Can. 1725.

4. Prorogation.

Prorogation may be defined as the extension of the competence or jurisdiction of a judge beyond its limits to persons or causes not otherwise falling under his competence or jurisdiction, which extension is made by the parties voluntarily submitting their case to him.

For jurisdiction to be prorogued by the consent of the parties four things are required; of these, two are required on the part of the judge whose jurisdiction is prorogued, and two on the part of the parties. On the part of the judge it is required (1) that he be in his own territory, and (2) that he be not *absolutely* incompetent to try the case of the parties, otherwise the parties would not be extending an already existing jurisdiction, but rather conferring new jurisdiction, which cannot be done by the consent of the parties nor by the wish of private citizens. As a consequence of the fulfillment of these two requirements, the judge, since his competence is not founded on any of the titles in Canons 1560-1568, is *relatively* incompetent to try the case submitted to him. Nevertheless, his decision holds, for the sentence passed by a relatively incompetent judge, though it is illicit, is *valid*.[68] On the part of the litigants it is required (1) that they consent to the judge not their own, knowingly and willingly, and not through error, and (2) that they be not prohibited by law from proroguing the jurisdiction of the judge, e. g., clerics cannot prorogue the jurisdiction of a lay judge.[69]

Certain cases do not admit of prorogation. Among these, three classes may be specially mentioned: (1) *cases of appeal,* since by their nature they should be brought to the Superior judge, it necessarily follows that no other judge can be approached unless he is the Superior of

---

[68] Cans. 1559, para. 2; 1692.

[69] Reiffenstuel, Tom. II, pp. 34, 35, nn. 129-134; Schmalzgrueber, Lib. III, Pars. I., Tit. 11, nn. 144, 146-150.

the judge from whom the case is appealed; (2) *in criminal cases,* because prorogation in these cases might pave the way for fraud and prove disadvantageous to the plaintiff or defendant; (3) *in spiritual cases,* including sacramental and non-sacramental cases, without the consent of the Bishop."[70]

A recent author gives it as his opinion that the New Code in Canon 1559, para. 1, has abolished the forum of prorogation. In confirmation of this opinion he alleges the exception made in Can. 1565, para. 2, "In which there is granted implicitly to each of the contracting parties the right to prorogue competence, for they are granted the power, limited however, to the actual drawing up of the contract, to choose the judge (*before whom they are to appear*). This concession, but especially the limitation annexed to it, shows that in all other cases outside of contracts, and even in contracts, outside the case of selecting a judge in the very act of making the contract, there is no permission given to choose the judge, or what is tantamount to this, the forum of prorogation is abolished.'"[71]

The Code does not speak explicitly of the abolition of the forum of prorogation, but it does speak implicitly of its retention. How can the validity of sentences passed by a relatively incompetent judge be otherwise explained? Now, prorogation, if anything, seems to be extended. It is no longer confined to four methods, as it was under the old law,[72] viz., (1) *person to person,* when persons mutually consented to subject themselves to a judge not their own; (2) from *cause to cause,* when the contending parties agreed to submit to a judge having limited jurisdiction in one kind of cases so that he might also try that part of the case which exceeded his jurisdiction; (3) from *time to time,* when the time set for deciding a case had elapsed, it might be protracted by the consent of the parties so that the same

[70] Schmalzgrueber, Lib. III, Pars. I, Tit. II, n. 145.
[71] Noval, *op. cit.,* p. 38.
[72] Cf. Reiffenstuel, *loc. cit.* nn. 124-128; Schmalzgrueber, *loc. cit.,* n. 143.

judge might settle the case; (4) from *place to place,* when a case was transferred to a place of the same jurisdiction, or of another judge's jurisdiction; if of the same jurisdiction, the consent of the parties sufficed; if to the jurisdiction of another judge, the consent of that judge was also required.

Canon 1669, para. 1, is an example of prorogation in actions and counter-pleas (*actiones et exceptiones*). If a plaintiff has several cases, either concerning the same object or different objects, he may bring them to the same court together, provided the tribunal is at least relatively competent to try the different claims. This is done to expedite trials, for it is useless to make several trials out of matter that can be decided in one trial.[73] The defendant, however, is allowed to put in a counter-plea to all the cases brought against him.

Canon 1688, para. 1, rules that *restitutio in integrum* should be sought from the judge who is competent with regard to the one against whom the injunction is asked, whether he be the plaintiff or the defendant. Under the old law, this competence was determined "by the general rules of competence,"[74] and under the New Code it is determined (1) for certain physical and moral persons by Canons 1556, 1557; (2) for other persons, acts or contracts by one of the titles laid down in Canons 1560-1568; (3) in judicial sentences by Canon 1906, which designates the competent judge to be the one who pronounced the sentence, except in cases where the regulations prescribed by law have been neglected, when the court of appeal is competent to grant the *restitutio.* But if none of these titles justifies the judge in hearing the case, and the parties submit to his jurisdiction, if he be only *relatively* incompetent, he can hear the case and render a valid decision.

---

[73] Cf. Schmalz. Lib. III, Pars. I, Tit. III, n. 9.
[74] Lega, Lib. I, n. 281.

Canon 1692 furnishes an example of prorogation in counter-charges or counter-pleas (*reconventiones*). It permits a counter-plea to be made before the judge before whom the main suit was brought, even though he may be delegated for one special case only, or may be otherwise incompetent, provided he be not absolutely incompetent. Noval, commenting on this Canon says that counter-pleas may be proposed to a relatively incompetent judge, "whose relative competence or jurisdiction is prorogued by the will of the legislator, as manifested by this Canon.'"[18]

---

[18] Noval, *op. cit.*, p. 235, n. 350.

III. ORDINARY COMPETENT TRIBUNALS.

1. Necessary Forum.

There are some causes which have a necessary forum. Under grave obligation, but not under pain of nullity, must this tribunal be approached, for other judges are relatively incompetent in such causes. This obligation is encumbent on the plaintiff and must be urged by the judge against the defendant, even though the latter be absent or unwilling to appear before that tribunal.

Causes pertaining to a necessary forum are as follows:

(1) Actions for recovering possession (*actiones de spolio*) must be tried before the Ordinary of the place in which the object is situated, i. e., the place in which are found the things, and we may even say the object of the rights, of which the plaintiff has been deprived.[76]

In every complete title to an object of right two things are necessary, the possession and the right of property. The term *quasi-possession* is used by the Code to indicate rights which are properly possessed, but are incorporeal, for example, the right of election.[77]

(2) Causes referring to a benefice, even a nonresidential benefice, have a necessary forum before the Ordinary of the place of the benefice. This Canon refers to the institution, conferring, suppression, union, or dismembration of benefices.[78] It also has reference to pensions and the *jus patronatus*, or the right to designate the person upon whom the office is to be conferred.

[76] Can. 1560, n. 1.
[77] Can. 1668, para. 2.
[78] Can. 1560, n. 2; institution, etc., of benefices is regulated by Cans. 1414-1447.

(3) Causes concerning the administration of ecclesiastical goods are to be tried before the Ordinary of the place where the administration is conducted.[79] By *ecclesiastical goods* are meant the temporal goods, both movable and immovable, and the temporal rights which belong to the universal Church, or to the Apostolic See, or to any other moral person in the Church.[80]

(4) Causes referring to inheritance or pious legacies have a necessary forum before the Ordinary of the domicile of the testator, unless those causes deal with the mere execution of the legacy, in which case the ordinary rules of competence are to be followed. Hence the execution of the legacy will pertain to the forum of the defendant, i. e., the forum of the person who is to be prevented from hindering its execution, or the person from whom it is sought to have the legacy carried out.[81]

The reason for this and for the other dispositions of Canon 1560 is that in the places therein mentioned proofs are more easily found.

[79] Can. 1560, n. 3.
[80] Can. 1497, para. 1.
[81] Can. 1560, n. 4.

2. Forum by Reason of Domicile.

There are, as already explained, different kinds of judges and courts in the ecclesiastical forum. Nevertheless contending parties cannot choose their own judge; the trial must be conducted by the proper judge, the judge who can exercise his jurisdiction against the accused, in other words, the competent judge. Moreover, as the defendant is generally brought to court against his will, it is necessary that the judge have the power to summon him and oblige him to appear. If in civil courts it was considered an essential requisite for the proper administration of justice to place territorial limitations to the exercise of jurisdiction, the same restrictions were likewise indispensable in the Church.

Of the ordinary titles by which an accused party comes under the jurisdiction of a certain judge, the first and most natural is that acquired by domicile.

Little interest was manifested by canonists in the question of domicile until the Fourth Council of Lateran. Contentious matters were settled on quite different principles. A delinquent was brought before the judge in whose territory the crime had been committed or the disputed object was located. Domicile was never a decisive test. Even Gratian never alludes to domicile as having any importance.

The foundation of the School of Bologna revived interest in the study of ecclesiastical law. As far as the question of domicile was concerned, for them the Roman *origo* meant the place of birth; they established a *domicile of origin,* entirely unknown in Roman law, and held that residence was as equally important as the intention in acquiring a domicile. The School exercised a great influence over canonists, but for a long time the latter refused to accept the erroneous views of Roman law held by the School. As time went on, the School became prominent and its teachings official, so that its influence was too strong to brook resistance. Hence we find Sanchez, a prominent canonist of the seventeenth century, conceding to residence the same importance as intention and making it one of the two absolutely essential elements.[52] With the admission of that principle, other points in the Roman theory were superseded. The *domicile of origin* gradually lost its importance, as did the ten years' test.

The theory of double or multiple domicile finds no favor in American or English law.[53] Canonists, on the contrary, admit the possibility of acquiring more than one domicile or quasi-domicile,[54] the determining factor being chiefly the intention with which one takes up an abode. Neither law recognizes quasi-domicile, nor do they admit that a person can ever be without a domicile; in other points, as a rule, civil legislation is in harmonious accord with ecclesiastical legislation.

Naturally, therefore, the New Code has placed first among the ordinary methods of choosing a forum that arising from residence. By reason of domicile or quasi-domicile any person may be summoned before the Ordinary of the place.[55] The Justinian Code gives us the definition of domicile as formulated by the Emperors Diocletian and Maximian, "Each one has his domicile in the place where he has established his home and business and has his possessions; a residence which he does not intend to abandon, unless called elsewhere, from which he departs only as a traveller and by returning to which he ceases to be a traveller."[56] The principal element constitutive of domicile is the intention to settle oneself in a place, this intention being deduced from the circumstances and conditions of installations. A domicile is acquired by staying in a parish or quasi-parish (parochial domicile), or at least in a diocese, Vicariate Apostolic, or Prefecture Apostolic (diocesan

---

[52] *De Matr.* III, 23-25.
[53] Encyc. Brit. (11th Ed.) art., *Domicile.*
[54] Gasparri, *De Matr.*, II, n. 1089.
[55] Can. 1561, para. 1.
[56] L. 7, Cod. X-40, *de incolis.*

domicile), to which stay is added the intention of remaining there permanently, if nothing calls one away. This intention is supplied by actual residence for ten full years.[87] There is a legal domicile, that imposed by law; for prisoners or exiles, in their prison or place of banishment; for a wife not legitimately separated from her husband, it is the domicile of her husband, if legitimately separated she can choose her own domicile;[88] for children under age or wards it is the domicile of the parents or guardians who have authority over them;[89] lastly, for whoever exercises a perpetual charge, e. g., a Bishop, it is the place where he discharges his functions. There is no mention of the *commoratio mensilis* which the *Ne Temere* had introduced, and which the Code has adopted with regard to matrimony.[90] In no other case does a monthly stay suffice for performing a legal act. Domicile or quasi-domicile decides the competent forum in all other juridical matters.

Domicile is lost by departure from a place with the intention of not returning, except for the provision made in Canon 93. The reason for this exception is evident from the juridical assumption that wives, minors, and the insane have no domicile of their own choice. When a wife legitimately separated from her husband for any of the reasons given in Can. 1131, para. 1,[91] is obliged to return either by a decree of the Ordinary or by the lapse of the specified time of separation,[92] she loses the domicile she may have acquired in virtue of Can. 93, para. 2.[93]

---

[87] Can. 92, paras. 1 & 3.

[88] Can. 93, para. 2; *S. C. C.*, Apr. 27, 1720; *S. C. De Prop. Fide*, Instr. 1883, n. 2.

[89] Cf. Can. 93, para. 1.

[90] Can. 1097, para. 1, nn. 2, 3.

[91] These reasons include affiliation with a non-Catholic sect; rearing the offspring in a non-Catholic spirit; leading a criminal and scandalous life; occasioning grave danger to the soul or body of the other consort; cruelty rendering a community of life very difficult; and other causes of a similar nature.

[92] Can. 1131, para. 2.

[93] "A wife may acquire a domicile provided she is legitimately separated from her husband."

3. Forum by Reason of Quasi-Domicile.

Neglected and obscure as was the idea of domicile, we find that the notion of quasi-domicile was still more obscure. No germ of the idea can be found among the Roman regulations. In fact, it was not until after the Council of Trent that the idea of quasi-domicile was generally accepted or that any serious effort was made to determine the necessary qualifications for securing it. The Council decided that for Catholics the assistance of the parish priest was necessary for the valid reception of matrimony.[64] Whether the parish priest alluded to was the parish priest of the place in which the marriage was celebrated, or of one or other of the contracting parties was not made sufficiently clear. Soon, however, the interpretation was accepted that the parish priest mentioned meant the parish priest of one or other of the parties.[65] And since it would often be exceedingly difficult, if not impossible, to have the marriage celebrated in the place of domicile, a sentiment arose in favor of a less stringent qualification to constitute the prospective bride or bridegroom a parishioner. Hence the decision that this qualification was either a domicile or a quasi-domicile.[66]

The rule thus made in regard to marriage was gradually adopted in other ecclesiastical matters, assuming in time the importance now given it in Canon Law. At first, its meaning was vague and nebulous. Canonists differed in their definitions, as might be expected; indeed, it was not until the last century that any universally approved definition was decided upon.

---

[64] Can. 1, Sess. 24, *de reform. matrim.*

[65] S. C. C. 1574.

[66] "Parochum proprium habendum esse parochum domicilii vel quasi domicilii contrahentium." *In Mutinen.* Matr., 18 Nov. 1702; Bened. XIV. Instit. 33, n. 6.

Sanchez, in 1592,[67] was the first to attempt a solution. The precise importance he attached to *intention* is somewhat obscure, but in all other particulars he is credited with having outlined the principles now accepted by Canon Law.

Fagnanus, half a century later, required little more than actual residence.[68] To him there seemed to be no reason for insisting on a period of "*six months*" or "*the greater part of a year*" as a necessary qualification. The sentiment in favor of six months' residence became more common, despite the able support given to Fagnanus by De Luca, some twenty years later. Benedict XIV, when Archbishop of Bologna, also attempted to settle the matter, for the peaceful adjustment of complicated cases in his own diocese.

It was not until 1867, when the Holy Office took the matter in hand, that any general principle was formulated. The decree published on June 7, 1867, comprised the following regulations:

1. To constitute a quasi-domicile two conditions are required, namely, residence and the intention of staying there for the greater part of the year.

2. From the very first day on which these conditions are verified a quasi-domicile has been acquired.

3. If the intention cannot be ascertained with certainty, one must have recourse to such indications as might lead to moral certainty; e. g., if one or both parties have resided in the locality for at least one month.

4. If such is the case, it is regarded by a presumption of the law that there existed the intention of remaining the greater part of the year, and that a quasi-domicile was acquired.[69]

---

[67] *De Matrimonio*, L. 3, Disp. 23.

[68] "Ut quis efficiatur parochianus et recipiatur ad sacramenta non requiri formalem translationem domicilii, sed sufficere simplicem habitationem de praesente" (n. 18).

[69] *Litt. Encycl. S. C. S. Off.*, 7 Junii, 1867, and 9 Nov., 1898 (ad Epp. Angliae et Stat. Foeder. Amer. Sept.) In the New *Collect. S. C. de Prop. Fide.*, nn. 1305, 2025.

The month's residence constituted a presumption of the law (*presumptio juris*), and determined the probative effect of an actual state of facts, when no evidence to the contrary was forthcoming. It never became a presumption of so absolute a character that no evidence was admissible in disproof of it (*presumptio juris et de jure*); in other words, it yielded when proof to the contrary was available.

An important exception was made to the above law for the United States. The Archbishop of Baltimore petitioned the Holy Office "to decree that those who pass from their own diocese to another, providing they remain in the latter for the space of one month, by that very fact, without any inquiry being made about their intention of remaining the greater part of the year, should be regarded as having acquired a quasi-domicile."[100] The Holy Office on November 25, 1885, decreed that "those passing from a place where the decree *Tametsi* binds into another—should be considered as having a quasi-domicile there for matrimonial purposes, provided they remain for a space of one month."[101] Two important departures were thus made from the general law; quasi-domicile was acquired by one month's residence, and the intention of staying was not deemed necessary.

In 1898 the same reply was given to the Archbishop of Paris, except that six months' actual residence was required instead of one.[102] On November 9, 1903, the Cardinal Archbishop asked and secured the privilege already granted to the United States. The original Paris concession was extended to Berlin on May 20, 1905. These decisions, however, referred to particular places only, and to the acquisition of a quasi-domicile for one particular purpose.[103] Other problems in theology and Canon Law depended upon general regulations

[100] *Acta et Decreta Conc. Plen. Balt. Tertii, p. cix.*
[101] *Idem.*
[102] *Collect. S. C. de Prop. Fide*, n. 2025.
[103] Decree *S. C. S. Off.* Jan. 26, 1903, in *Nouv. Rev. Theol.*, T. 39, p. 516.

as modified by the Decree of 1867 and subsequent decisions.

Quasi-domicile is now acquired by staying in a parish, quasi-parish, diocese, vicariate-apostolic or prefecture apostolic, which stay is either joined to the intention of remaining there for the greater part of the year, at least six months, if one is not called away, or is in reality protracted to the greater part of the year.[104] A minor after the completion of his seventh year and a wife not legitimately separated from her husband may acquire a proper quasi-domicile.[105] Those having a quasi-domicile are regarded as subjects of the local authority, just as are permanent residents, with this difference, they may, if they so choose, use their rights in their own domicile.

Quasi-domicile is lost on the same conditions as domicile itself.[106]

The reason for the forum of domicile and quasi-domicile is this: although the Church's jurisdiction extends throughout the world, still to avoid confusion over jurisdiction, and to secure the proper administration of justice, which requires that a judge have some knowledge of the persons and things he is to judge, there have been rightly established, besides the tribunals of the Holy See, inferior tribunals, exercising their authority within territorial limits.[107] Hence persons, things and rights which are contained within that territory are subject to the judge of the territory.

This jurisdiction a judge can exercise over his subjects even though they are absent from his territory.[108] The judge himself, outside his territory, cannot exercise judicial power, whether ordinary or delegated, unless he be forcibly expelled from his own territory or be hindered in exercising jurisdiction there.[109] To

[104] Can. 92, para. 2.
[105] Can. 93, para. 2; *S. C. C.* Jan. 31, Feb. 21, 1835.
[106] Can. 95.
[107] Cf. Can. 201.
[108] Can. 1561, para. 2.
[109] Cf. Cans. 201, 1637.

exercise authority in these circumstances the judge has the right to requisition the assistance of another tribunal, namely, that of the territory in which his subject is residing, in all that pertains to the citation and examination of the parties and witnesses, etc.[110]

4. Forum of a Stranger in Rome.

A peculiar right is vindicated to the City of Rome. A *peregrinus*—he who is travelling outside his domicile, and quasi-domicile, though he still retains them[111]—who is sojourning in Rome, even for a short time, can be cited to appear in that city as in his own domicile, but he has the right of calling on his home, i. e., of asking that he be sent back to his own Ordinary for trial.[112]

The tribunal granted to a stranger in Rome is a relic of Roman law, a part of the ancient Roman concept of domicile expressed by Cicero in these words: "I hold that all citizens have two homes, one of nature, the other of the city" (i. e., Rome).[113] Very often a stranger might become involved in a legal controversy at Rome when it was vitally important that he hasten homeward to attend to his commercial interests. Thus it would be a great boon to the foreigner to have his case quickly decided. Some foreigners were permitted to institute legal action at Rome. But for those not so privileged the increasing number of cases necessitated, about the middle of the third century, B. C., the creation of a new pretor to deal with cases in which foreigners were involved. He was called the *praetor peregrinus,* as distinct from the *praetor urbanus* before whom those cases came in which two Roman citizens were engaged.

Gregory IX embodied the same concept in canonical legislation: at the Apostolic See, "which is the mother

---

[110] Can. 1570, para. 2.
[111] Can. 91.
[112] Can. 1562, para. 1.
[113] *De Legibus,* II, 2.

and teacher of all churches, (a defendant) can rightly be compelled to appear there (at Rome) against his adversaries, unless he had come for another just and necessary cause, which if he alleges, he has the right of having the case pleaded at home.'"[114] As under the Decretals, so now by the New Code, any cleric or layman who is in Rome may be summoned there.

The right, "*jus revocandi domum,*" is not the same as that of declining the forum, "*jus declinandi forum.*" In the latter the defendant does not recognize the competence of the judge, and declines his tribunal because he is not subject to the jurisdiction of that judge; in the former the competency is admitted. Since the Roman Pontiff is the ordinary judge of all the faithful, the defendant cannot decline his tribunal, although he can ask to have the trial conducted at home. Under the old law this favor was granted only when the stranger had come to Rome "for a just and necessary cause.'"[115] The New Code makes no mention of this conditional clause, and we may conclude that it is no longer a requisite condition. We may, however, admit what the same writers[116] say concerning two other reasonable conditions for refusing the use of the "*revocatio.*" They deny the right where there would be danger in delay, or if the stranger had committed a crime in the City of Rome.

By "*Rome*" we do not mean here the determined city which is called by that name, but rather the place in which the Roman Pontiff resides, whether it be Rome or some other place. Wherever the Pope resides, there is "*Rome,*" there he has his tribunal. In like manner with the ancients, there was Rome where the Roman Emperor resided—"*ubi Imperator, ibi Roma.*"

Hence it follows that the judge of the Roman Curia is the ordinary and competent ecclesiastical judge of

---

[114] Cap. 20, X, *de foro comp.*, II, 2.

[115] Reiffenstuel, Tom. II, Tit. II, nn. 109-112; Schmalzgrueber, Lib. III, Pars. I, Tit. II, n. 28.

[116] Reiffenstuel, *loc. cit.*, n. 113; Schmalzgrueber, *loc. cit.*

all the faithful staying in Rome. This holds true, despite the contrary statute of the Council of Trent, ordaining that all causes, in whatsoever manner pertaining to the ecclesiastical tribunal, should in the first instance be tried and decided only by the Ordinaries of the place.[117]

5. Forum by Reason of Residence in Rome For a Year.

Suppose a person staying at Rome is summoned to appear before the Ordinary of his domicile, can he object to being tried by his own Ordinary? His objection would not be sustained by the old law, because if a person had obtained a forum in two places, e. g., when he possessed two true domiciles, it was left to the option of the plaintiff which court to choose.[118]

The common law in this respect was amended by the Constitution of Eugene IV, so that officials of the Holy See and others staying in Rome for some special business could not be cited outside the Roman Curia.[119] But since the administration of justice was very often frustrated by trials held outside the place of domicile, Paul V in the Bull, *Universi agri,* 1611, decided that this privilege could not be obtained, except by those "who had resided in the Curia for at least one continuous year." The Council of Trent restricted the privilege granted by Eugene IV, decreeing that "those privileges usually accorded on the strength of the Constitution of Eugene IV to residents in the Roman Curia are by no means to be understood as applying to those who obtain ecclesiastical benefices by reason of the aforesaid benefices, but they remain subject to the jurisdiction of their Ordinary, all customs to the contrary notwithstanding."[120] It likewise expressly abrogated this privilege

---

[117] Conc. Trid., Sess. XXIV, cap. 20, *de ref.;* Gregory XIII, Bull, *Ad Romani,* 1574; Schmalzgrueber, *loc. cit.,* n. 27.

[118] Lega, *loc. cit.*

[119] Cap. 1, *de privilegiis,* V, 7, *in Extravag. Com.*

[120] Conc. Trid., Sess. XXIV, cap. 2, *in fine.*

in the case of pastors staying at Rome *in fraudem legis*, and ordered them to reside in the church of their benefice.[121]

Under the new legislation, one who has lived in Rome for one year has the right of declining the court of his Ordinary and of demanding that his case be tried before the tribunals of Rome.[122] In this case he is tried before the tribunals of the Vicariate of Rome, not before those of the Holy See, for he is summoned, not in his capacity as one of the faithful, but as a privileged Roman citizen.

6. Forum of *Vagi*.

Vagi, wanderers, have their proper tribunal in the place where they are actually staying,[123] even though they have made up their minds to settle in another place.[124] Vagi are those who have no fixed domicile or quasi-domicile, or who, having definitely abandoned one domicile or quasi-domicile, have not as yet acquired another.[125] They are obliged to observe both the general and the particular laws in effect at the place where they are staying,[126] and they are also subject to the pastor or to the Ordinary of the place where they are staying.[127] This latter disposition of the New Code has solved a much disputed question.

With regard to the competent tribunal of *vagi*, no innovations have been introduced by the New Code. Its regulations are in keeping with the old law as usually accepted and consistently applied by the commentators. Justice and the common welfare demand that *vagi* also have a competent judge before whom they are obliged to appear for infractions of the law, even when they

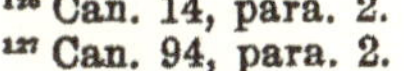

[121] Conc. Trid., Sess. XXIII, cap. 1, *in fine*.
[122] Can. 1562, para. 2.
[123] Can. 1563.
[124] Reiffenstuel, Tom. II, p. 26, n. 45.
[125] Can. 91.
[126] Can. 14, para. 2.
[127] Can. 94, para. 2.

no longer dwell in the territory in which those infractions were committed. It is eminently fitting, therefore, that *vagi* can be apprehended and summoned for trial wherever they are found.

7. Forum of Religious.

Religious are subject to the forum of the place in which their house is situated.[128] Under the general name "*religious*" come those men or women who have taken vows in any religion.[129] If the religious are not exempt, or in those cases in which they are not exempt, their competent tribunal is that of the Ordinary of the place in which their house is situated; otherwise it is that of the religious Ordinary having jurisdiction over that house.

In the first instance: If a dispute arises between individual exempt religious of the same order or congregation, provided their Constitutions do not ordain otherwise, the judge of the first instance is the Provincial, or if the monastery be autonomous, the local Abbot.[130] Unless the respective Constitutions provide otherwise, a civil case pending between two provinces must be tried, in the first instance, by the Superior-General himself or by his delegate; if the controversy is between two autonomous monasteries the competent judge is the Superior Abbot of the monastic congregations.[131] If the contention arises between physical or moral religious persons of different religions, or between individual religious of non-exempt congregations or lay institutes, or between a religious and a secular cleric or a lay person, the judge in the first instance is the local Ordinary.[132] It is understood in this last-mentioned case that both litigants are in the same diocese.

---

[128] Can. 1563.
[129] Can. 488, n. 7.
[130] Can. 1579, para. 1.
[131] Can. 1579, para. 2.
[132] Can. 1579, para. 3.

If they are not, the other rules of competency are to be followed, namely those mentioned in Canons 1564-1568.[153]

In the second instance: When the causes of religious are tried in the first instance by a judge of the secular clergy, if it be before the tribunal of a Suffragan Bishop, appeal is made to the Metropolitan. If the case was tried in the first instance by the Metropolitan, appeal is made to the court of that local Ordinary whom the Metropolitan, with the approval of the Holy See, has chosen once for all as the court of appeal. From cases first tried before an Archbishop who has no suffragans, or before a local Ordinary, such as a prelate or abbot *nullius*, who is immediately subject to the Holy See, appeal is made to the nearest Metropolitan, chosen once for all, with the approval of the Holy See.[154]

When cases of religious are tried in the first instance before judges of their own order or congregation, for all cases tried by the Provincial the tribunal of second instance is Superior-General, and in cases tried by the local Abbot appeal is made to the Superior Abbot of the monastic congregation.[155] We must not forget, however, that the Roman Pontiff remains the supreme judge in all matters for the whole Catholic world, and that, instead of leaving a case to these tribunals, he may pronounce judgment himself, or entrust the case to judges delegated by him.[156] Wherefore, any cause, civil or criminal, may be appealed to the Apostolic See by the faithful, and religious also, in any stage of the trial and from any phase the trial may have taken.[157] But recourse to the Apostolic See does not suspend the exercise of jurisdiction of the ordinary or delegated judge who has already commenced the trial. Hence he may

---

[153] Aug., VII., p. 37.
[154] Can. 1594, paras. 1, 2, 3; Can. 285.
[155] Can. 1594, para. 4.
[156] Cf. Can. 1597.
[157] Can. 1569, para. 1.

proceed with the trial and pronounce final sentence, unless he has been duly informed that the Holy See has called the case before its own court.[138]

8. Forum by Reason of the Location of the Object.

The fourth ordinary method of choosing a tribunal, as laid down by the Code, is that by reason of the location of the object.[139] By reason of the location of the litigious object, *ratione rei sitae,* one may be sued in any place where a real action is brought against him, on account of the location in that place of the object. This is true not only with regard to immovable property, but also movable property, provided the latter remains permanently, or at least for some time in the place.[140]

Three reasons are given why a person may be tried by the judge of the territory where the object is located, even though he is not otherwise under his jurisdiction: (1) in a *real* action—that which directly and immediately follows the thing—the object merits more consideration than the person. (2) In such a place the case is easier to prove and the execution of the sentence is attended with less difficulty, hence justice demands that an object be defended where it is located. (3) To do otherwise would not be a just withdrawal of the trial from the place in which the object has experienced jurisdiction and protection.

As a rule, all persons can be summoned for trial before the judge of the place in which the object is situated. They do not, of course, become absolute subjects of such a judge, but subjects in so far as the object—the principal motive for the real action—is concerned.

---

[138] Can. 1569, para. 2. The difference between appeal and recourse is explained in Can. 1889.

[139] Can. 1564; C. 3, 20, X, *de foro competente,* II, 2.

[140] Cod. Just., L. III, Tit. 19, C., *ubi in rem actio.*

In the place where the object is situated the defendant can be summoned by a *real* action only, and not by a *personal* action, that is, by an action against the thing and not against the person. The reason is evident. A *real* action follows the object, not the person, hence nothing prevents the defendant, as far as his person is concerned, from subjection to the jurisdiction of the judge of contract. In a *personal* action the opposite takes place, the action follows the person, not the object. Hence, the plaintiff about to institute a personal action should do so before a judge to whom the person of the defendant cited is subject. Therefore the judge of the place where the object is located cannot pass a sentence which would directly affect the person of the defendant; he may not excommunicate or suspend him or declare him contumacious, but only declare that the thing or property in dispute be given the complainant.

As a general rule, personal property is governed by the law of the domicile of the owner, irrespective of the situation of the property. By a legal fiction, personal property is supposed to adhere to the person of the owner, and unlike real property, to be governed by the law of the place where the owner is domiciled, and not by the law of the place where the property is situated. This doctrine, embodied in the maxim, *mobilia ossibus inhaerent*, grew up in the early Middle Ages, when movable property consisted chiefly of gold and jewels, which could be easily carried from place to place, or secreted in spots known only to the owner.

An interesting question here presents itself: can the defendant be prosecuted in a real action in the place where the object is situated, when he cannot be found therein?

Opinions of minor importance say no.[141] Arguing from the text that an inheritance is to be sought where he who is prosecuted has his domicile or where the hereditary objects are situated, if he lives there, they

[141] Cf. Schmalzgrueber, Pars. I, Tit. II, n. 53.

hold that if he does not live there, or is not found there, the action to recover the inheritance will have no effect on him. Furthermore, it is argued, it would appear unreasonable to have the defendant taken from his domicile to the place where the object is situated with a loss to his estate. Another reason alleged is that the forum where the object is located is comparable to that of the contract, and as in the latter the defendant cannot be prosecuted unless found there, neither can he be prosecuted in the place where the object is located, unless found there.

The more common opinion, and that generally followed in practice, is that the judge in the place where the object is located can proceed against an absent person by a real action only. On his refusal to obey the judge's citation to appear in court the judge can attach the property of the defendant and put the plaintiff in possession of the controverted object.

This method of procedure is more reasonable, for if, by reason of the location of the object, an absent person could not be summoned to the place in which the object was located, the location of the object would not constitute a separate and distinct forum. Again, when we are dealing with things, things should take precedence over persons. Finally, in the place where the object is located the trial can be more easily and expeditiously prosecuted than in a place far removed from that object.[143]

---

[143] Schmalzgrueber, *loc, cit.;* Reiffenstuel, Lib. II, Tit. II, nn. 98-104.

9. Forum by Reason of the Contract.

One of the most striking differences to be found in a comparison between a primitive and a highly developed legal system is the relative importance of the law of contracts. In modern times the central subject of the whole body of the law is that of contracts. In early systems contract law is practically limited to that of bailments and executed sales. The simple living conditions and the primitive state of society gave no occasion for the creation of a complicated system of contract law.

The act of the parties in entering into a contract in a particular place, in the absence of anything shown to the contrary, sufficiently indicates their intention to contract with reference to the laws of that place. They thereby become subject to the judge of the place of contract; and the contract itself, as to its nature, interpretation, validity and enforcement, is to be governed by the law of the place where it was made, unless the contracting parties clearly signify in the contract their intention of subjecting themselves to another judge.

The reason for such a law is evident. In Roman law,[148] the laws of contracts, while substantially the same throughout the empire, were nevertheless qualified and modified by local enactments. When a merchant of Rome, Africa or Spain entered into a contract in his own province, he was presumed to be cognizant of the laws of the place where he was, and to expect that his contract was to be judged and carried into effect according to those laws; and the merchant with whom he dealt, if a foreigner, was presumed to have submitted himself to the same laws, unless he had taken care to stipulate for a performance in some other country, or had in some other way, excepted his particular contract

[148] Rom. Law on Contracts found principally in *Corp. Jur. Civilis*, Lib. V, Tit. I. D. *De judiciis; ubi quisque agere vel conveniri debeat.*

from the laws of the province where the contract was made. Hence the rule that the validity of a contract is governed by the law of the place where the contract was entered into.

Canon Law likewise regulates that one may be tried by the Ordinary of the place in which the contract was made or must be fulfilled.[144] A contract may be defined to be an agreement by which one or more persons place themselves under obligation to one or more persons to give, do, or omit something. The word *"contract"* is taken in its widest sense, and means not only contracts proper, but also quasi-contracts, or even tacit agreements, such as occur in business transactions, and from which can spring an obligation of the natural law.[145]

Three reasons are alleged to show the reasonableness of such a forum. (1) It avoids expense and inconvenience on the part of the creditors in instituting proceedings before the judge of the debtor's domicile, very often a great distance from the place where the contract was made. (2) In the contracting place the contract is more justly viewed in its peculiar circumstances, than if the trial took place where the debtor has his domicile. (3) The contracting parties have implicitly or explicitly imposed upon themselves the obligation either of paying their debts where they were contracted or of their undergoing trial if they are not paid. However, the plaintiff still retains the option of bringing the defendant to trial either in the place of the contract or in the place where he (the defendant) has his domicile, for the forum acquired by the contract does not do away with the domiciliary forum.

Contracts are generally determined by obligations and circumstances, hence the Code permits the contracting parties to state in the contract itself the place where the obligation is to be declared, fulfilled, or urged, and in which the absent parties can be cited and prosecuted.[146]

---

[144] Can. 1565, para. 1; C. 17, 20 X, *de foro comp.*, II, 2.
[145] Reiffenstuel, *loc. cit.*, nn. 80-82.
[146] Can. 1565, para. 2.

The permission herein contained shows that when a judge is not specifically designated, an absent person can neither be cited nor prosecuted by reason of the contract.

This is a change from the regulations in force under the old law, according to which an absent person could be cited, but if he refused to obey, no trial could be instituted. The Decretals permitted the judge of the place of contract to cite the absent party, and if he contumaciously refused to appear, to place the plaintiff in possession of property the defendant might have in the territory of the one citing, or to decree that the plaintiff should be given possession by the Ordinary of another diocese of property owned in that diocese by the same defendant, in order that the latter might appear in court. He could not, however, pass any sentence affecting the person of the defendant, e. g., excommunication, nor could he directly condemn him for the debt, for that also concerned his person.[147]

But the Code permits both contracting parties, *when drawing up the contract*, to choose a tribunal before which they can be tried; *after the contract has been made*, no legal remedy is conceded. No mention is made of the aforesaid provisions of the old law, hence, these may be said to have lost their force. There is really no need for them, for if a contracting party should neglect to use the faculty granted him by the New Code against the absent party whom he wishes to have tried, he has but himself to blame.[148]

The question naturally arises, who acquires a forum in the place of contract? We reply that any person contracting in a place, acquires there a forum, providing, of course, he is *de jure* able to make a contract. Hence a court attendant would acquire a forum by virtue of a contract entered into by him, and so would a stranger, if he delayed sometime in the place of the contract or

[147] C. 17, X, *de foro comp.*, II, 2; c. 1, *de foro comp.*, II, 2, in VI°.
[148] Noval, *op. cit.*, paras. 83, 84.

undertook any business there; for, notwithstanding the fact that they are not residents, they can be brought to trial in the place of the contract. This is true also of an absent person who has contracted either through himself or through an agent, and the absent person can be there brought to trial where he contracted through his duly constituted agent.

This is also true of a person who has the privilege of responding only in a certain place, e. g., where he has his domicile, because it is taken for granted that by contracting in another place he subjects himself to the judge of that place and renounces his privilege. But those who have such a privilege granted them by the common law are excepted from this rule.

It would seem as if clerics were also exempted from this rule, since a cleric cannot without the permission of his own Bishop extend to himself the jurisdiction belonging to another, even though that other be an ecclesiastical judge. The New Code, however, does not make any reference to the old law prohibiting clerics from subjecting themselves with regard to contracts to Ordinaries other than their own.[149] Moreover, it ordains that contentions between religious individuals or corporations of different communities, or between religious or secular clerics or laymen are tried in the first instance by the local Ordinary.[150] Hence we think that a cleric, or even an exempt religious, who contracted with another cleric, religious or secular, or a layman, could be cited to appear before the judge of the place of contract, provided it be an ecclesiastical judge before whom the cleric is to appear.

When does a *peregrinus* obtain a forum in the place of contract? If he delays there for some time, according to approved authors, a forum by reason of the contract is acquired. The reason is that by this fact he is considered as having tacitly promised to liquidate

[149] C. 18, X, *de foro comp.*, II, 2.
[150] Can. 1579, para. 3.

his debts or appear where he delays a longer time or conducts his business. If he departs immediately after making the contract, we must distinguish; either those with whom he contracted knew that he would depart in a short time, or they did not know it. *If they did not know it,* they can, by reason of the contract, make him appear in the place where the contract was made, because the probable ignorance of those contracting with a *peregrinus* ought not be held against them; and furthermore, the *peregrinus* was at fault by neglecting to inform them of his personal status. *But if they did know* that he would depart in a short time, they could not make him appear in the contracting territory by virtue of the contract alone. According to rule he should be made to appear in the place of his domicile.

As a general rule the contracting parties can be made to appear in the place of the contract, if they can be found there, provided there was no different arrangement made between the parties and there is no opposition from the particular laws of the locality. Here might be considered the bringing to trial of persons absent from the place of the contract. It can be done (1) if the place of the contract is the same as the absent person's domicile, because he is subject to the judge of that place, who can summon him, even though absent, to trial; (2) if the absent person promised to appear for trial in the place of contract, and at the same time renounced his domiciliary forum; (3) if the trial deals with the absent person giving an account of his administration. A distinction is here made between a public and private administration, to the effect that an absent person can be summoned in the former case but not in the latter. The weight of authority, however, supports the opinion that he can be summoned in either case; (4) if the trial, by reason of a contract, has already been begun before the judge in the place of the contract, and one of the parties has since died, his heirs, should the opposing party so wish, will be obliged to reopen and continue the trial, even though they are not in the place of the contract.[151]

We might also consider those instances in which the contracting party, even when present in the place of contract, cannot be tried there. Two cases are cited: (1) if the contracting parties mutually agreed not to summon each other for trial in the contracting place should the terms of the contract be unfulfilled; (2) if the merchant selling to a stranger who he knows will depart at once, does not demand cash payment, the credit of the purchaser is considered to perdure, and payment cannot be sought in that place.[152]

10. Forum in the Place Where Crime has Been Committed.

By reason of the commission of a crime, a person falls under the competence of the ecclesiastical judge of the territory where he has committed the crime, even though in other respects he is not subject to that judge.[153]

The principle of the forum by reason of crime prevailed under the later Roman Empire. Valentinian and Valens in 373, and later Theodosius I, are quite explicit on this point: "It behooves the judgments of crimes to be there conducted where the deed is said to have been committed. The trials of strangers are also subject to the present laws."[154] Constantius and Constans in 355 made an exception in cases of Bishops, stating that they could be tried only by other Bishops.[155]

---

[151] Cf. Schmalzgrueber, *loc. cit.*, nn. 39-42.
[152] *Idem*, n. 43.
[153] Can. 1566, para. 1.
[154] *Cod. Theod.*, IX, 1, 10; IX, 1, 16.
[155] *Id.* XVI, 2, 12.

The Church adopted the same regulation. It was incorporated in the Decretals,[156] affirmed by the Council of Trent,[157] and now it is embodied in the New Code.

It is eminently proper that crimes should be punished in the place where they have been perpetrated, partly that the punishment of those found guilty may serve as an example to deter others from committing crime, and partly because the necessary proofs are more easily obtained there. Moreover, a crime, which in ecclesiastical law is an external and morally imputable violation of the law to which is added a canonical sanction, at least an indeterminate one,[158] is a disturbance of the order of the place. The purpose of punishment is to restore that order. It is fitting, therefore, that the accused should be tried and public reparation made in the place where the crime was committed.

The defendant may be a resident (*incola*), a visitor (*advena*), a stranger (*peregrinus*) or a *vagus*, providing he is not exempt from the jurisdiction of the local Ordinary, e. g., the cases of actual rulers of nations.[159] Clerics are also comprised in this method of obtaining a forum. Cardinals, Legates of the Holy See, and Bishops are subject to the Roman Pontiff.[160] Regulars are likewise exempt from the jurisdiction of the local Ordinary, except (1) when they have committed a crime outside their house and their Superior, knowing of the crime, does not punish them, they may be punished by the local Ordinary;[161] (2) all other matters in which religious are subject to the local Ordinary.[162]

How can the ecclesiastical judge of the territory in which the crime was committed proceed against the perpetrator of the crime? The response depends on whether

---

[156] C. 19, C. 11, q. 1; c. 1, 2, 7, 18, C. III, q. 6; C. 13, 14, 20, X, *de foro comp.*, II, 2.

[157] Conc. Trid., Sess. VI, *de ref.*, c. 3; Sess. VII, *de ref.*, c. 14; Sess. XIV, *de ref.*, c. 5.

[158] Can. 2195.

[159] Can. 1557, para. 1, n. 1.

[160] *Id.* nn. 2, 3.

[161] Can. 616.

[162] Can. 619.

the delinquent is present in the place or whether he has departed, for although the competence of such an Ordinary is not based on the delinquent's presence nor on his possession of property there, nevertheless, one of these two things is required before the Ordinary can efficaciously proceed against the delinquent. Hence:

(1) If the delinquent is at the time actually in the place or territory where the crime was committed, the ecclesiastical judge of the territory has full power to try and punish him. He can even pass sentence of dismissal from his benefice or ecclesiastical office, should the nature of the crime warrant it, even though the benefice or office be situated in another diocese. In the latter case execution of the sentence belongs to the judge or Bishop in whose territory the benefice or office is located.[163]

(2) If the delinquent is absent from the territory in which the crime was committed, the Ordinary of this place has the right to summon him and to pronounce sentence on him.[164] The right to summons mentioned here is not limited to the drawing up and the conveying of the citation.[165] It is a citation properly so-called, i. e., it includes the right to apprehend the person sought, and for this purpose a courier may be sent within the boundaries of another diocese, if the judge deems it expedient and commands him to do so.[166] The citation to be executed may also be sent, together with extradition papers (*litterae remissoriae*), to the judge in whose territory the person to be cited is found.[167] The latter judge is bound to send him to the judge who issued the citation.

A defendant who has been duly summoned and does not appear in court either personally or by proxy may be declared to be in contempt of court,[168] if the summons

[163] Reiffenstuel, *loc. cit.*, n. 48; Schmalzgrueber, *loc. cit.*, n. 61.
[164] Can. 1566, para. 2.
[165] Cf. Can. 1719.
[166] Can. 1717, para. 2.
[167] Can. 1570, para. 2.
[168] Can. 1842.

was lawfully issued[169] and the defendant offered no legitimate reason for his non-appearance in court.[170] A second summons may be issued with the threat of ecclesiastical penalties in order to force the contumacious defendant to be obedient.[171] If he still refuses to appear for trial the judge of the place where the crime was committed may proceed against him.[172] *"In eum,"* the Canon says, making no distinction as to whether such procedure should take the form of a personal or a real action; hence, where the law makes no distinction, we should make none.

Under the old law, if the delinquent had left the place before he was cited to appear for trial, no personal action (*actio personalis*) could be brought against him by the judge of the territory where he committed the deed, i. e., the judge could not pass a sentence nor issue a mandate directly affecting the person of the defendant. But the promoter of justice might bring a real action (*actio realis*) against him. The judge could deprive the defendant of his possessions located in the place where the crime was committed, should he have refused to make satisfactory compensation. If he had no possessions in the place where the crime was committed, but had them elsewhere, the judge of that place could be requested to put the plaintiff in possession of the defendant's property. The reason was that the defendant was still obliged to satisfy for the injury and damage he had caused, and his property might be taken to compensate those injured by his misdeeds.[173]

Moreover, the defendant could be compelled by the Ordinary of his domicile or quasi-domicile, if the judge of the place where the crime was committed requested

---

[169] In accordance with Cans. 1711-1716.
[170] Can. 1843, para. 1.
[171] Can. 1845, paras. 1, 2.
[172] Can. 1566, para. 2.
[173] Schmalzgrueber, *loc. cit.*, n. 61.

it, to appear before the latter judge for trial. If he appeared, both personal and real actions might be taken against him; but if he did not appear, a real action only could be taken.[174]

IV. SPECIAL COMPETENT TRIBUNALS.

1. Matrimonial Causes.

Matrimonial procedure in the primitive ages of the Church was for the most part informal. Christian matrimonial law was without precedent in the ancient world, and consequently it manifests a decided departure from the defensive procedure in their courts. Nevertheless, from the very beginning, through the harrowing ages of persecution and the threatening periods of barbaric invasion, as well as in the days of rigorous formality against the so-called Reformers of the sixteenth century, the essential requirements of justice in the process were faithfully observed.

Owing to the increasing number and importance of matrimonial causes in the fifth and sixth centuries, we find contemporary legislation restricting matrimonial jurisdiction to Provincial Synods. "If they cast aside their wives before they are condemned in a trial, and before they have brought their causes to the Provincial Bishops, let them be excluded from the communion of the Church and the assembly of the people because they have soiled the faith and marriage."[175]

The period from Gregory the Great to Innocent III is remarkable for laying the foundations of statute law. We find that the right of the Church to adjudge matrimonial causes was unchallenged by the princes or people of this epoch. An increase of matrimonial litigation was caused by the gradual formation of the laws governing impediments. Gregory the Great fixed the

---

[174] Reiffenstuel, *loc. cit.*, nn. 56-62.
[175] *Concilium Agathense* (a. 506) Can. 25, apud Mansi.

decrees of consanguinity within which matrimony was forbidden.[176] Innocent III changed to the fourth degree the previous law which prohibited marriage within the seventh degree of kindred.[177]

The diriment character of solemn vows was early recognized, and during this time legislation in councils was enacted to that effect.[178] Another departure was that, while matrimonial procedure hitherto had been more or less identified with the regular ecclesiastical procedure, which in turn was moulded upon the process of civil law, during this period its peculiar character became more pronounced and special exceptions for its procedure were introduced.

From the time of Innocent III a solemn and intricate process prevailed until the *Dispendiosam* of Clement V, who introduced the "*summary*" process, allowing the judge in the adjudication of matrimonial causes to dispense with the formalities and solemnities of the judiciary. The Council of Trent, in its clear definitions of doctrine on matrimony and its rigorous scrutiny through tribunals trying violations of the Church Law, maintained unsullied the unity, sanctity and indissolubility of matrimony.

After the reforms made by the Council of Trent, the most celebrated enactment was that of Benedict XIV, Constitution *Dei miseratione,* Nov. 3, 1741, in which are to be noted especially the institution of the "defender of the matrimonial tie," and the necessity of two concordant decisions on the invalidity of a marriage. This Constitution was followed by many instructions of the Holy See, unfolding and perfecting its meaning, notably the *Instruction of the Holy Office,* June 20, 1883.

---

[176] II *Conc. Romae,* a. 600; cf. also *Conc. Lat.* IV c. 35, 8, 3; Can. 7, 17, 19; c. 35, q. 5, Can. 2.

[177] Conc. Lat. IV, c. 8, "*Prohibitio quoque copulae conjugalis quartum consanguinitatis et affinitatis gradum de cetero non excedat.*"

[178] Sub Callixto II in *Conc. Lat.* 1123, Can. 24, statutum est "*ut irrita omnino forent ea conjugia.*" This was confirmed by Innocent II, 1139, Lateran Council, Can. 40, dist. 29, qu. 1, "*Hujusmodi copulationem matrimonium non esse censemus.*"

This brief survey of the development of matrimonial procedure affords sufficient proof for the statement that the Church has always defended and enforced in her legal tribunals her sublime doctrine on marriage, even when such defense meant the loss of nations to the faith—all this constitutes one of the brightest pages in her glorious history.

(a) Competence of the Church and the State.

Hence, after unwinding the cerements of antiquity, we arrive at the conclusion that the matrimonial bond between Christians has always been regarded as indissoluble.[179] Spouses were never permitted of their own volition and private authority to dissolve marriage, even though there existed a diriment impediment known to all. The trial of such matrimonial causes has always been claimed by the competent ecclesiastical authorities.

Matrimonial causes, strictly so-called, are those which concern the nullity or dissolution of the matrimonial bond to permit another marriage, or those which concern the essential effects of matrimony. In Canons 1960-65 the New Code deals with the competent forum in matrimonial causes. The first Canon speaks in a general way of the competent forum, determining the competent tribunal of those who may be at the same time members of the Church and of the civil society, namely, that matrimonial cases between baptized persons belong by proper and exclusive right to the ecclesiastical judges.[180]

The Church *alone* is competent. Christian marriage is a sacrament and a contract, but as a contract it cannot be separated from the sacrament, nor can we admit of any real distinction between the two.[181]

---

[179] Conc. Trid., Sess. XXIV, *De matrim.*, cans. 1, 5; New Code, Cans. 1013, 1110 and notes.

[180] Can. 1960; Conc. Trid. loc. cit., can. 12; *Instr. S. C. de P. F.*, 1883 (Collect. n. 1587).

[181] *Instr. S. C. S. Off.*, July 6, 1817 (Collect. n. 725).

Hence, any modifications of the contract at the same time affect the sacrament; conditions required for the validity of the contract are likewise required for the reception of the sacrament, and persons hindered from making the contract are also to be rejected as ministers of the sacrament.

By the exercise of jurisdiction over the sacramental character of matrimony the contract is not changed, for where there is no sacrament there is no valid contract. Since, for baptized persons, the sacrament and the contract are identical, those controlling the sacrament should supervise the contract, and those laying down conditions necessary for the validity of the sacrament should determine the conditions necessary for the validity of the contract.

As the Church alone of its native right controls the administration of the sacraments, matrimonial trials, because of their intimate connection with the sacramental dignity, must be brought before the ecclesiastical judge. "Whatever belongs, either of its own nature or by reason of the end to which it is referred, to the salvation of souls or the worship of God is subject to the power and judgment of the Church."[182]

This right, too, belongs *properly* to the Church because of her divine origin and constitution. No assent or connivance is required of the civil power, nor can the civil power in any way alter this right.[183] Among jurists there is a commonly accepted axiom to the effect that he who has made a law should judge litigations referring to that law, or that he who has legislative power in a certain thing should have judicial power in the same thing. Canon 1960 plainly enunciates this fact in claiming for the Church the proper and exclusive right to judge matrimonial cases between baptized persons. Trent taught under pain of anathema, that matrimonial cases pertain to ecclesiastical judges.[184]

---

[182] Encycl. *Immortale Dei*, Leo XIII, Nov. 1885.
[183] Encycl. *Arcanum*, Leo XIII, Feb. 10, 1880.
[184] Sess. XXIV, can. 12.

Pius VI holds that the statement of Trent is to be interpreted in an exclusive sense, "The words of the canon are so general that they comprehend and include all causes. The spirit or reason of the laws is so extended as to leave no room for exception or limitation; for if these causes belonged solely to the judgment of the Church for no other reason than because matrimony is really and truly one of the seven sacraments, since this quality of the sacrament is common to all matrimonial cases, all these cases should be tried only by ecclesiastical judges."[165]

If one party is baptized and the other is not, "it would seem at first as if the principle, '*Actor sequitur forum rei,*' should be applied, so that, if the defendant is an infidel, the competent judge is the lay judge; if the defendant is a member of the faithful, the competent judge is the ecclesiastical judge. But that principle serves only to determine what lay judge is competent in a civil case, or what ecclesiastical judge is competent in an ecclesiastical case, while here the question is whether the ecclesiastical judge is competent, or the lay judge. * * * We think the ecclesiastical judge is competent, no matter which party is defendant or plaintiff. For the marriage in question, although you may deny that it is a sacrament properly so-called, will be nevertheless by its nature a sacred thing, which, by reason of the faithful party, belongs to the Church."[166] Should both of the parties be infidels, the competent judge is certainly not the ecclesiastical judge, but the lay judge.[167]

Conflicts may and do arise between the ecclesiastical and civil authorities, so that one jealously guards what the other rejects; the civil power often holds in contempt and punishes that which the Church blesses and

[165] Pius VI epist. *ad. Episc. Matulensem*. Heuser, *De Potestate Statuendi Impedimenta*, pp. 11 sqq.
[166] Gasparri, *De Matrim.*, II. n. 1456.
[167] *Id.* n. 1455.

Wherefore no inferior judge can institute proceedings in cases of dispensation from a ratified marriage, unless the Holy See has granted him faculties for that purpose.[199] However, inferior judges may be indirectly empowered to institute a trial which may lead to a dispensation from a ratified marriage. In cases of impotency, which a judge is entitled to take cognizance of in virtue of his own authority, when the existence of impotency cannot be proved, but merely the fact that the marriage has not been consummated, all the acts of the case should be forwarded to the Sacred Congregation of the Sacraments, which may use them to pass judgment on the ratified but not consummated marriage.[200]

3. The Holy Office. Cases which have reference to the Pauline Privilege are reserved to the Sacred Congregation of the Holy Office.[201] Here only the Pauline Privilege is mentioned, while in Can. 247, para. 3, matters concerning the impediments of disparity of worship and mixed religion are likewise reserved to the same Congregation. The principal reason why these dispensations have been committed to the Holy Office is because that Congregation is the designated custodian of the faith, to conserve and defend which necessitates the prevention of such marriages, when it can be done, and when it cannot, that the proper precautions be observed.

This jurisdiction, however, is only disciplinary, and no deduction can be made either from the Constitution *Sapienti consilio,* or from the *Normae peculiares* to warrant the inclusion of judicial power. In the Constitution it says that the faculty belongs exclusively to the Holy Office to take cognizance of those things which

---

[199] Can. 1963, para. 1.

[200] Can. 1963, para. 2; *Instr. S. C. S. Off.*, Aug. 6, 1890 (Collect. n. 1737): "Quando vero ex serie actorum impotentia concludenter probari non poterit, constabit tamen morali certitudine matrimonium minime consummatum fuisse, et causas adesse quae pontificiam dispensationem super matrimonio rato et non consummato suadeant, integra acta transmittantur ad S. Sedem, una cum precibus quibus hujusmodi dispensatio postulatur."

[201] Can. 1962.

concern the Pauline Privilege and impediments of disparity of worship and mixed religion;[202] no mention being made of undertaking the judicial trials which can arise from those sources. The *"Normae peculiares,"* in explaining the provisions laid down in the Constitution, deal only with dispensations from such impediments, especially in Note 6, where, after confirming the judicial power of this Congregation in crimes of heretics, as to these impediments it mentions only the power of dispensing.[203]

Hence, in practice, it would seem that these causes should be referred to the Sacred Rota. But at times the Sacred Rota will have to suspend judgment and approach the Holy Office to obtain some declaration reserved exclusively to the competence of this Congregation; for example, a marriage of a non-baptized and a doubtfully baptized person is attacked. The cause is to be judged by the Sacred Rota. If the doubt is a *dubium facti,* it settles the doubt; if it is a *dubium juris*—one concerning the essentials of baptism—the Sacred Rota will refer the doubt to the Holy Office. Having received the reply of the Congregation, the Sacred Rota will judge accordingly as to the validity of the marriage.

The same more or less can be said of the Pauline Privilege. Everything pertaining to the requisite conditions for using this privilege, to the dispensations from the interpellation to be made, etc., belongs to the Holy Office. But concerning the question of the mere fact, whether before the marriage was contracted the interpellation had been made by the converted party, or whether a dispensation from making the interpellation had been granted, the Sacred Rota will decide.[204]

---

[202] Const. *Sapienti consilio,* para. 1, n. 1°, 5; n. 3°, 3.
[203] *Normae peculiares,* cap. VII, art. 1, nn. 4°, 6°.
[204] Ojetti, *De Romana Curia,* pp. 55, 56.

4. Congregation for the Propagation of the Faith.

Ecclesiastical provinces and dioceses subject to the Congregation for the Propagation of the Faith refer matrimonial causes to that Congregation, which in turn must refer them to the competent Congregation or Tribunal.[205]

5. The Congregation for the Oriental Church enjoys for Oriental rites all the faculties which other Congregations possess for the Latin rite, except those pertaining to the Congregation of the Holy Office in virtue of Can. 247.[206] To the Congregation for the Oriental Church belong all matrimonial controversies of the Oriental rites, and these it settles in a disciplinary manner. Those which, in its opinion, require a judicial trial are sent to the Tribunal designated by the Congregation.[207] No mention is made of the Sacred Rota, because the Sacred Rota might not always be competent to deal with oriental customs.

6. Diocesan Courts. In other matrimonial causes the competent judge of the first instance is the judge of the place where the marriage was celebrated, or where the defendant has a domicile or quasi-domicile, or, if one of the parties is a non-Catholic, where the Catholic party has a domicile or quasi-domicile.[208] Under the old law that Bishop was competent in matrimonial cases in whose diocese the husband had a domi-

---

[205] Can. 252, para. 4; Pius X Const. *Sapienti consilio,* para. 1, n. 6°, 4.

[206] Can. 257, para. 2; Pius IX Const. *Romani Pontifices,* Jan. 6, 1862 (Collect. n. 1223).

[207] Can. 257, para. 3; *S. C. Consist.,* Nov. 12, 1908, ad. VI. "Utrum Congregatio pro Negotiis rituum orientalium valeat. etiam in posterum concedere dispensationes matrimoniales mixtae religionis ac disparitatis cultus. Resp. Affirmative, excepto tantummodo privilegio Paulino, quod pertinet ad Congregationem S. Officii."

[208] Cans. 1964, 1572.

cile.[209] Hence, all cases of nullity, other than the three species mentioned in Can. 1962, arising either from one of the diriment impediments or from defective consent or non-observance of the prescribed form, and cases concerning the prohibitive impediments, separation, and legitimation of offspring are tried by the Ordinary of the diocese, because he is the *judex ordinarius* of the place.

Besides the Bishop of the diocese, the term "ordinary judge" also embraces Abbots and Prelates *nullius*, Vicars and Prefects Apostolic, Vicars-Capitular or Administrators,[210] and the Official chosen by the Bishop.[211] The Vicar-General is not included, unless he has been deputed Official.[212] Inferior prelates do not fall under the category of Ordinaries and therefore have no right to try such cases,[213] and under the old law Abbots and Prelates *nullius*, were directed to refer their matrimonial causes to a neighboring Bishop.[214]

Two qualifications are given by the Code in deciding the competent judge. The first is the *ratio contractus* or the place in which the marriage was celebrated. Before the New Code much doubt was attached to the validity of a sentence passed by a tribunal thus selected. No mention of this method was made in the Austrian Instruction or in that of the Congregation for the Propagation of the Faith, 1883, although excellent authority supported it. But now this reason may be invoked at any time, for the fact of having contracted marriage in a certain place remains. The second qualification is the domicile of the defendant. Equal to the domicile in this case is the quasi-domicile, and no preference may be claimed for either.

---

[209] Wernz, *loc. cit.*, n. 736; *Instr. S. C. de P. F.* Pars. I, n. 2 (Collect. n. 1587).

[210] Can. 198.

[211] Can. 1573, paras. 1, 2.

[212] Can. 1573, para. 1.

[213] Conc. Trid., Sess. XXIV, cap. 20.

[214] Conc. Trid. *loc. cit.*, Bened. XIV, Const. *Dei miseratione*, Nov. 2, 1741, (Collect. n. 332).

According to the New Code, the wife generally follows the court of her husband.[215] The Instruction of 1883[216] makes a twofold exception, which is implicitly admitted by the Code. If a husband and wife have been legitimately separated, and the former wishes to have the marriage annulled, he must do so before the tribunal of the Ordinary in whose diocese the wife has her domicile or quasi-domicile, because by a separation she may obtain her own domicile.[217] If the wife demands the annulment, she must do so before the tribunal of the Ordinary of the diocese in which her husband has his domicile. The other exception is in case of desertion. If the husband maliciously deserts his wife, she may institute proceedings in the court of the Ordinary in whose diocese she has her domicile. But if she deserts her husband, he may bring the case to the tribunal of the diocese in which he has his domicile. After the judicial citation has been made, a change of either party's domicile does not necessitate a change in tribunals.

In cases of mixed marriages, as well as of disparity of worship, one competent judge is decided by the domicile or quasi-domicile of the Catholic party.[218] This was stated in the decree of the Holy Office, "Spouses in cases of mixed marriages are subject to the Bishop in whose diocese the Catholic party has a domicile; and when both are Catholics, because the heretical party has returned to the Church, they are subject to the Bishop, in whose diocese the husband has his domicile."[219] To this decree must be added another decree of the Holy Office. "But when the case concerns the contraction of a mixed marriage with a heretic divorced from a heretic

---

[215] Can. 93, para. 1.
[216] *Instr. S. C. de P. F.*, 1883, Pars. 1, para. 2 (Collect. n. 1587).
[217] Can. 93, para. 2.
[218] The judge in the place of contract is also competent.
[219] June 30, 1892 (Collect. n. 1799).

by a sentence of the civil court, the Bishop of the domicile of the Catholic party is entitled to judge concerning the free status of the contracting parties.'"[220]

In cases of appeal from the first sentence which declared a marriage null and void, the defender of the bond must within the time fixed by law[221] appeal to the higher tribunal; and if he neglects this duty he may be compelled thereto by the authority of the judge.[222] The appellate tribunal is the one immediately higher,[223] except for the provision made in favor of the Sacred Rota when it concurs in the second instance with ordinary tribunals.[224] Since marriage cases may be reopened at any time provided new proofs are offered, in the third, or even in the fourth instance, the competent tribunal is the Sacred Rota.[225]

The Code now exhorts the judge to endeavor to bring about a peaceful settlement before legal procedure is instituted. If the court is asked to declare a marriage invalid for want of consent, arising, e. g., from error, compulsion or fear, or conditional consent, the judge should first of all try by opportune admonitions to induce the party whose consent is said to have been deficient to renew the consent. If the essential form of the marriage was wanting, or marriage was made invalid by a diriment impediment of a kind from which the Church can and usually does dispense, the judge should endeavor to induce the parties to renew the consent in the legal form, or ask for a dispensation.[226]

---

[220] June 23, 1903 (Collect. n. 2170).
[221] Can. 1881.
[222] Can. 1986.
[223] Can. 1594, paras. 1, 2, 3.
[224] Can. 1599, para. 1, n. 1.
[225] Cans. 1989; 1599, para. 1, n. 2.
[226] Can. 1965.

(c) Administrative Procedure.

As a rule, a declaration of nullity cannot be arrived at, in a diocesan court, without a judicial process held in accordance with the formalities prescribed in Canons 1960-1989. But there are certain cases in which the Ordinary can proceed without going through the form of a matrimonial trial. The Ordinary may declare a marriage null and void, provided the defender of the bond has intervened, when it is proved by unimpeachable evidence, that a marriage was rendered invalid by the impediment of disparity of cult, sacred orders, solemn vow of chastity, existing marriage bond, consanguinity, affinity, or spiritual relationship, and when there is equal certainty that no dispensation from these impediments has been obtained. In these cases the formalities mentioned thus far may be omitted and the Ordinary, having summoned the parties, and having given the defender of the bond an opportunity to examine the case, may declare the nullity of the marriage.[227]

Against this declaration of nullity the defender of the bond is bound to appeal to the judge of the second instance if for good reasons he thinks the impediments mentioned in Canon 1990 do not certainly exist, or that probably dispensation from them had been obtained before the marriage. If he appeals, the acts of the case are to be sent to the judge of second instance, who should be reminded in writing that this is a case excepted from the ordinary rules of a canonical trial.[228]

The judge of the second instance shall, with the co-operation of the defender of the bond, examine whether the first sentence should be confirmed or whether

---

[227] Can. 1990.
[228] Can. 1991.

the case is to follow the ordinary form of canonical procedure. If the appellate judge disapproves of the extra-judicial opinion, the case is returned to the court of first instance for a judicial trial.[229]

With reference to Canon 1990 the Papal Commission for the Authentic Interpretation of the New Code has recently decided the following cases:

(1) If two Catholic parties have contracted marriage before the civil magistrate only, without observing the *Tametsi* or the *Ne temere,* in places where these laws are binding, and wish to contract marriage anew *"in facie Ecclesiae,"* or wish to have their civilly contracted marriage revalidated, the local Ordinary (or the pastor after having consulted the local Ordinary) may declare the first marriage null and void without a formal trial and without the intervention of the *defensor vinculi,* after having made the investigation prescribed in Can. 1019, i. e., after having ascertained the free status of the couple—that no other impediment except the formerly clandestinely and therefore invalidly contracted civil marriage is in the way.

(2) The same rule is to be applied in cases of mixed marriage contracted invalidly in a non-Catholic church under the same condition, provided the Catholic party wishes to contract a new marriage with a Catholic.

(3) The same rule applies in cases where apostates from the Catholic faith have contracted an invalid civil marriage for the same reason, and, now repentant, wish to contract a new marriage with a Catholic party *"in facie Ecclesiae."* But in each and every one of these cases a civil divorce must have first been obtained.[230]

[229] Can. 1992; *A. Ap. S.* 1 Dec., 1919.
[230] *A. Ap. S.,* Vol. XI, p. 479 (Oct. 16, 1919).

2. Procedure in Ordination Cases.

Among the causes which require special rules for trial, ordination causes come last, not indeed in dignity, but because of their infrequent occurrence. Such causes are threefold:

(1) Those in which the obligations contracted in ordination are impugned, for example, the observance of celibacy or the recitation of the Divine Office. Force and fear (*vis et metus*) may be alleged to avoid the obligations attendant on valid ordination, and if the compulsion and lack of approval are legitimately proved in accordance with Canons 1993-1998, the recipient may be returned to the lay state by the sentence of the judge, without the obligations of celibacy and the recitation of the canonical hours.[231]

(2) The validity of ordination may also be attacked because of the lack of intention or of the power of orders on the part of the minister or the non-reception of baptism or absence of consent in the person ordained.

In any of these cases a petition must be sent to the Congregation of the Sacraments.[232] The defect of intention or consent is very difficult to prove *in foro externo,* hence the Sacred Congregations very seldom declare ordinations invalid on that score.

(3) Finally, the validity of ordination may be questioned because of a substantial defect of the sacred rite, affecting either the matter of the order conferred, for example, if, in the ordination rite to the priesthood, the second imposition of hands did not take place, or the form of the order conferred, that is, the prayers or words corresponding to the matter.

---

[231] Can. 214, paras. 1, 2.
[232] Can. 1993, para. 1.

Here the question of validity is more readily answered, because the rites are external actions performed in the presence of witnesses. If the validity of ordination is disputed because of a substantial defect of the sacred rites, the petition must be sent to the Sacred Congregation of the Holy Office;[233] and rightly so, because the matter is connected with faith and morals, the care of which is entrusted to this Congregation.[234] The Congregation shall decide whether the case is to be tried in a judicial or a disciplinary manner.[235]

If the judiciary form is selected, the Sacred Congregation refers the case to the court of the diocese to which the cleric belonged at the time of his ordination, or, if the ordination is impugned because of some substantial defect of the sacred rite, to the tribunal of the diocese in which the ordination took place. The various instances of appeal are governed by Canons 1594-1601.[236] The case is returned to the diocesan tribunal, not for information, but for judicial proposal, trial and definition; and the tribunal must be composed of three judges, if it is a question of the bond (*vinculum*) of ordination.[237]

Another course is open to both Congregations. Either may, if it thinks it opportune and the case permits, refer the question to the Sacred Rota for a judicial trial.[238] Cases thus referred are judged by the Sacred Rota in the first instance. The Sacred Rota, however, does not give the dispensation. It judges only of the validity or invalidity of the ordination, then sends its decision to the proper Congregation, which gives or does not give the declaration of nullity, according to the decision of the Sacred Rota.

If the disciplinary form is selected, the Sacred Congregation shall settle the question after having received

[233] Can. 1993, para. 1.
[234] Can. 247, para. 1.
[235] Can. 1993, para. 1.
[236] Can. 1993, para. 2.
[237] Can. 1576, para. 1, n. 1.
[238] Cans. 247, para. 3; 249, para. 3.

the necessary information from the competent diocesan court.[239] In furnishing this information (*processus informativus*), diocesan courts propose and determine the question, investigate facts, examine proofs, and inquire into the challenges (*exceptiones*). A verdict or sentence is not required, for this is reserved to the Sacred Congregation. Where the disciplinary form alone is followed, dispensations from irregularity to sacred ordination in doubtful or more difficult cases, or where the favor asked would scarcely redound to the glory of an ecclesiastical assembly, petitions concerning invalid ordination or its obligations, or exemption from them require a plenary session of the Congregation to give a decisive vote.[240]

The cleric himself, as well as the Ordinary to whom he is subject or in whose diocese he was ordained, may question the validity of an ordination.[241] The reason is evident, for it concerns the public good that no one be considered a sacred minister who is not one. Only the cleric who thinks he has not contracted the obligations arising from ordination can seek exemption from these obligations,[242] for the assumption of the obligations involved is directly personal, and the measure of an action should be the extent of the thing concerned.

As far as they can be adapted to this purpose, those rules enacted for trials in general, Canons 1556-1924, and those laid down in Canons 1960-1992, for matrimonial cases, are to be observed in the trial of cases concerning ordination.[243] A novelty in Canon Law is the

---

[239] Can. 1993, para. 3.
[240] *Ordo Servandus in S. Congregationibus, Tribunalibus, Officiis Romanae Curiae*, Sept. 29, 1908, para. 11. *Normae peculiares*, Cap. VII. Art. III, n. 11, b.
[241] Can. 1994, para. 1.
[242] Can. 1994, para. 2.
[243] Can. 1995.

defender of the ordination bond, who has the same rights[244] and duties[245] as the defender of the marriage bond.[246]

When a cleric has brought suit for the purpose of being freed from the obligations arising from sacred ordination, even though he does not attack its validity, and *a fortiori* if he does attack it, he is provisionally prohibited from the exercise of orders. This prohibition is to prevent him from exercising orders which he may not have. It is not penal, and if the cleric affected by it were to illicitly exercise the functions proper to his order, he would not incur the irregularity mentioned in Can. 985, n. 7.

To free a cleric from the obligations attached to sacred orders, if the case is considered in a judiciary manner, two conformable sentences are required.[247] Trials concerning the validity of an ordination can never be considered closed, but may be reopened whenever new evidence warrants such action.[248] Concerning appeals in ordination trials, the regulations laid down in Canons 1986-1989 for appeals in matrimonial trials are to be observed.[249]

3. *Privilegium Fori,* or Privileged Forum of Clerics.

The *privilegium fori, privilegium clericale,* or, as it is called in English law, the *benefit of clergy,* had its origin in the pious regard paid by Christian princes to the Church in the fourth and following centuries. The exemptions which they granted to the Church were principally of two kinds: (1) Exemptions of *places* consecrated to the service of God from criminal arrest, which

[244] Cans. 1969, 1983, para. 2, 1984, para. 1.

[245] Cans. 1968, 1986, 1991, cf. etiam Const. *Si datam,* Bened. XIV, Mar. 4, 1748.

[246] Can. 1996.

[247] Can. 1998, para. 1. cf. *Instr. S. C. C.* 1838, apud Sentis, *Decretales Clem.* VIII., p. 41 sq.

[248] Can. 1903.

[249] Can. 1998, para. 2.

was the foundation of the right of sanctuary; (2) exemptions of the *persons* of clerics from criminal process before a secular judge in a few particular cases. This was the true origin and meaning of the *privilegium fori*, by which ecclesiastics are exempt from all secular jurisdiction, so that they may not be brought before civil tribunals, nor be condemned nor imprisoned by the sentence of secular judges.

The purpose here is not only to claim for the Church the exclusive right to judge spiritual or mixed causes, but also to show the incompetence of secular tribunals, with reference to the person of clerics, even in a criminal cause. It certainly does not seem proper that civil judges have the right to take cognizance of the causes of clerics when even ecclesiastical things are removed from their jurisdiction and when it is repugnant for the faithful to see judged those whom they justly call their fathers and judges, and by whom they believe they can be bound and loosed not only on earth but also in heaven.

It was not until the distinction in Christian society between the clergy and the laity became more pronounced that the circumstance of one of the parties being a cleric was made a reason for referring that cause to an ecclesiastical tribunal, and a foundation for the jurisdiction of such a tribunal. In his ordinance of February 5, 330, the Emperor Constantine confirmed its usage. In it he says, "Clerics who were unjustly brought before civil tribunals by heretics should be freed; and moreover, in accordance with the custom of the East, they should not be summoned to appear before tribunals, but should enjoy complete immunity."[250]

Concerning the same question, in 376, we find the law of Valens, Gratian and Valentinian: "That which is the custom in civil causes obtains likewise in ecclesiastical affairs; so that if in certain dissentions and crimes of minor importance there are any pertaining

---

[250] *Cod. Theod.*, L. XVI, T. II, C. 2.

to the observance of religion, they are to be heard in their own places and by the synods of their own diocese, those being accepted which constitute a criminal action to be heard by ordinary and extraordinary judges or by illustrious authority.'"[251] This law, according to the Breviary of Alaric,[252] deals only with civil causes and penal causes of minor importance having a connection with religion; it has nothing to do with causes exclusively ecclesiastical, and it attributes criminal causes to the competence of the lay judge.

Probably in 384, Valentinian, Theodosius and Arcadius decreed that the competent judge in ecclesiastical causes was the ecclesiastical judge.[253] By "*ecclesiastical causes,*" they intended, according to St. Augustine,[254] not only those within the Church, but also those concerning the persons of ecclesiastics.

Several of the early councils of the Church made it incumbent upon the clergy to refer their disputes to their own magistrates. Some canons of the fourth and fifth centuries threaten with excommunication a Bishop or priest bringing suit, civil or criminal, before a secular magistrate.[255] Whether these canons applied only to those cases in which both disputants were clerics was not made clear. But all cases to which a cleric was a party, either as complainant or defendant, were tried before the episcopal tribunal. Justinian, too, favored this interpretation in his provision that civil suits against ecclesiastics be carried only before the Bishops. At the same time he provided that a party dissatisfied

---

[251] *Id.*, L. XVI, T. XXIII, C. 2.

[252] Interpr. legis, *eodem loco.*

[253] Const. *Sirmond.* 3, *Append. Cod. Theod.* Mommsen ed.

[254] *Epist.* XXI, n. 2, Migne P. L. XVI, 1045.

[255] Some of these canons were confirmed by the emperor and were thereby raised to the rank of imperial laws, e. g., The Council of Carthage, in 397, threatened with excommunication any cleric accusing another before the secular tribunals. The Fourth General Council of Chalcedon, in 451, repeated this decree, which was approved by Marcianus and was incorporated into the law of the Roman Empire.

with a sentence might apply to the secular magistrate, not as to an appellate court, but as to one of co-ordinate jurisdiction. If each court handed down different judgments, the case was ultimately referred to the emperor.

From that time this immunity, often accepted by Christian princes,[256] has always been claimed by the Popes, as their canons testify. But modern legislations do not recognize this right of the Church, which has been compelled to inflict punishments in order that the right be observed. Hence, after having condemned in the Syllabus those who pretend "that the ecclesiastical tribunal for trials of clerics in temporal things, whether civil or criminal, should be entirely abolished, even without consulting the Apostolic See, and in spite of its objection,"[257] Pius IX excommunicated also those who, directly or indirectly, compel lay judges to bring before their tribunal ecclesiastical persons, contrary to canonical regulations; likewise those who promulgate laws or decrees in opposition to the liberty or rights of the Church.[258] Pius X[259] extended further this censure by excommunicating, reserved to the Holy See in a special manner, the layman or ecclesiastic, man or woman, who, without the authorization of the Church, should cite or compel a cleric to appear, even as a witness,[260] before a public secular tribunal.

The Constitution *Apostolicae Sedis* and the *Motu Proprio* of Pius X maintain the principle of clerical immunity with regard to secular tribunals; but this common right, which the Pope cannot abolish in an absolute manner, suffers exceptions. These emanate either from concessions of the Holy See, as for example, those made

[256] Thomassin, P. II, L. III, C. 102 et sqq.

[257] *Syllabus* of Pius IX, para. V, prop. 31; Allocut. *Acerbissimum*, Sept. 27, 1852, and Allocut. *Nunquam fore*, Dec. 15, 1865.

[258] Const. *Apostolicae Sedis*, Pius IX, Oct. 12, 1869, para. 1, n. 7 (Collectanea n. 1348). See also explanation of the same in *Litt. Encycl. S. C. S. Off.*, Jan. 23, 1886, and *S. C. de Prop. Fide*, May 17, 1886 (Collectanea nn. 1652, 1656).

[259] Motu proprio, *Quantavis diligentia*, Oct. 9, 1911.

[260] Reply of the Holy Office to the Bishop of Larino, in *Il Monitore Ecclesiastico*, Mar. 31, 1912.

in concordats, or from legitimate customs to the contrary, or from special authorizations. This authorization is not necessary when the custom is legitimately prescribed, according to the declaration of the Secretary of State.[201] But in all these cases the civil judges act as delegated by the Church.[202]

Canon Law still claims for clerics and ecclesiastical persons a privileged forum, by which are reserved exclusively to ecclesiastical judges the temporal cases, civil or criminal, of clerics, unless a special exception has been made.[203] Purely ecclesiastical causes are not here dealt with, for in them clerics and lay people are alike subject to ecclesiastical authority alone. Here are considered only those causes temporal in themselves, e. g., wills, inheritance, or patrimony, but because of their connection with the person of a cleric, which is held to be sacred, they acquire a certain spiritual aspect.

In the privileged forum of clerics the question of clerical immunity is restricted to their exemption from secular judges and tribunals. Hence is omitted the questions of the extent of clerical exemption from civil laws and the obligation of observing those civil laws consonant with the dignity of a cleric.

Clerics in all cases, both civil and criminal, must be summoned before the ecclesiastical judge, unless for some countries special provision has been made.[204]

Cardinals, Legates of the Holy See, Bishops, even titular ones, Abbots and Prelates *nullius,* the supreme heads of religious bodies approved by Rome, the major officials of the Roman Curia, in reference to affairs belonging to their office, cannot be sued in secular courts without permission of the Holy See. All other clerics and religious, who enjoy the privileged forum, cannot be sued in a civil court without permission of the

[201] Reply of the Secretary of State to the Minister of Belgium, December, 1911. See the *Canoniste Contemporain,* May, 1912.

[202] Cap. "*Decernimus,*" 2, *de Judiciis.*

[203] Cans. 120, 614, 680, 1553, para. 1, n. 3.

[204] Can. 120, para. 1.

Ordinary of the place where the case is to be tried; the Ordinary, however, should not refuse such permission, if the plaintiff is a lay person, especially after his attempts to affect an agreement between the parties have failed.[265]

If clerics are sued in a civil court by one who has not obtained permission, they may appear in court because they are forced to obey the summons in order to protect themselves against more trouble, but they shall inform the Ordinary from whom permission should have been obtained.[266]

The Church inflicts certain punishments on those who violate the *privilegium fori.* They are of different degrees according to the rank of the person against whom the offense is committed.

An excommunication *latae sententiae* reserved to the Holy See in a special manner is incurred by him who dares bring before a lay tribunal, without permission from the Apostolic See, one of the Roman Cardinals, a Legate of the Holy See, or one of the higher officials of the Roman Curia, in connection with matters pertaining to his office, or his own Ordinary. The term, *"Legates of the Apostolic See,"* includes in the present Code, not only nuntios and internuntios, but also Apostolic Delegates.[267]

The higher officials of the Curia are, besides the Cardinals, those whom the Pope appoints directly without concursus; in the Congregation of the Holy Office, the Assessor and the Commissary; in the Sacred Congregation of the Sacraments, the Secretary and three Subsecretaries; in the Congregation of Council and Religious, the Secretary and Sub-secretary; in the Consistorial Congregation, the Assessor and substitute; in the Congrega-

---

[265] Can. 120, para. 2; cf *Acta Apos. Sed.* 15 Oct. 1917.
[266] Can. 120, para. 3.
[267] Can. 267; Pighi, *Censurae Sententiae Latae,* n. 28.

tion of Rites the Secretary and substitute, etc. These are protected by this censure in matters arising from their office; in other matters they are in the same condition as other ecclesiastics.

The penalty is an excommunication reserved to the Holy See in a simple manner, when the ecclesiastic brought before the court without papal authorization is a Bishop other than the offender's own Ordinary, even a merely titular Bishop or an Abbot, a Prelate *nullius*, one of the major Superiors in a papal institute, i. e., a religious organizaton which has received the approval of the Holy See.

The major Superiors are the Abbot primate, Abbots who are Superiors of monastic congregations, Abbots of independent monasteries, the Superiors-General of any religious congregation, the Provincial and their Vicars, and all others who have the same jurisdiction as Provincials.[268]

When any person entitled to the privilege of the court other than those mentioned above is brought before the civil judge without the permission of the Ordinary of the place, the penalty is suspension from office, reserved to the Ordinary and to be incurred *ipso facto*, if the offender is a cleric; if he is a layman, he shall be punished by the Ordinary according to his guilt.[269] Under the old law the punishment was excommunication for all, now for the laity it is *suitable penalties*, (*congruae poenae*).[270] Those entitled to the privileged court are all clerics, that is, all who have received at least first tonsure, and also all religious.[271] The word "*religious*" is here taken in its widest sense, including even lay brothers and sisters and novices, and those who

[268] Can. 488.
[269] Can. 2341.
[270] Pius IX, Const. *Apostolicae Sedis*, Oct. 12, 1869, para. 1, n. 7; Can. 2341.
[271] Cans. 108, 614.

lead a common life after the manner of religious even without vows,[272] whether all of the above mentioned be men or women.[273]

Under the discipline of the *Bulla Coenae* these penalties were incurred by the judges or officials, not by private persons, parties or plaintiffs. Under the Constitution *Apostolicae Sedis* they were not incurred by private persons or by judges but by legislators or higher officials, not by the *trahentes* but by the *cogentes trahere*, by persons in authority who freely, *a nullis coacti*, forced the judges to act. The *Motu Proprio, Quantavis diligentia*, applies the censure also to private persons suing clerics in the civil courts.

Canon 2341 is lacking in the clause which concerns legislators or other Superiors who may impose upon judges the obligation of summoning ecclesiastics. These are affected by Canon 2334. By Canon 2341, those are punished who bring ecclesiastics before the civil magistrate, the *trahentes*. Both judges and plaintiffs are or may be *trahentes;* and therefore, they are the ones affected by the penalties.

The *privilegium fori* must be in force in the place in order that the penalties be incurred. After the publication of the *Quantavis diligentia*, the Holy See declared that because of pre-existing customs or concordats it did not apply to Germany, Belgium and Holland; and it was generally held that for similar reasons it did not apply to France, Ireland and English speaking countries. The same holds true for the present law. In the United States by custom and also by the laws enacted in the Plenary Councils of Baltimore, especially the Third, it has remained forbidden for priests to sue other ecclesiastics in civil courts, but laymen have been at least implicitly authorized to do so.[274] Therefore, priests who would, without the regularly required permission, bring ecclesiastics before lay judges, would in-

[272] Can. 680.
[273] Can. 490.
[274] *Acta et Decreta Conc. Plen. Balt. Tertii*, n. 84.

cur penalties enacted by the common law, excommunication or suspension from office; but laymen may be considered as having the Ordinary's necessary permission by custom and implicit general concession.[375]

Lower clergy and other persons enjoying the *privilegium fori*, if they are not exempt from episcopal jurisdiction, can and ought to be summoned in the first instance before the Bishop who, by one of the titles in Canons 1560-1568, is their proper ecclesiastical judge in civil and criminal trials. Regulars and other exempt religious are subject to their religious Superiors.

To summon them before a lay judge it is always necessary to obtain the permission of the Ordinary of the place in which the trial is held.[376] This permission the Ordinary should not refuse to grant without a just and grave reason should the plaintiff (*actor*) be a lay person, and especially when the Ordinary's efforts to settle the difficulties of the contending parties have proved futile.[377] Nevertheless, if religious are summoned by a person who has obtained no permission, because of necessity, and to avoid greater evils, they ought to obey, after informing the Superior from whom permission was not obtained.[378]

Modern states no longer recognize the *privilegium fori*, even for Cardinals, for in recent times they have often been summoned to appear before the civil tribunals in Rome.[379] The civil and criminal causes of other clerics also, according to the secular law, belong to the lay courts, and only with respect to the purely spiritual con-

---

[375] *Eccles. Rev.* Sept., 1912, p. 312 ff; Ayrinhac, *Penal Legislation*, pp. 254-263.

[376] Can. 120, para. 2.

[377] Idem.

[378] Can. 120, para. 3.

[379] Cf. Brandi, *I Cardinali di S. R. Chiesa nel Diritto Publico Italiano*, Roma, 1905.

ditions of their station and office are they subject to their Bishops. The Church, however, still maintains in principle the *privilegium fori* for all clerics, even for those who have been tonsured or who are in minor orders, provided that they wear the clerical garb, and either already serve in a church or are preparing in a seminary or university for the reception of higher orders.[290]

V. COMPETENT ROMAN TRIBUNALS.

1. The Roman Pontiff.

The Roman Pontiff has received from Christ supreme authority over the whole Church, and it follows from this very fact that he, in the direction of the faithful to eternal salvation, possesses full jurisdiction and all its attributes. He alone, or together with a Council called by him, can make laws for the universal Church, abrogate them or derogate from them, grant privileges, appoint, depose, judge or punish Bishops. He is the supreme judge by whom all causes are to be tried; he is the supreme judge whom no one may try.

(a) Immunity of the Roman Pontiff. The immunity which all clerics enjoy by virtue of the juridical independence of the Church, is irreconcilable with submission of ecclesiastical persons to the civil power, either in virtue of the natural and divine laws in what pertains to the exercise of their spiritual ministry, or in virtue of the ecclesiastical law, founded on the divine, in what constitutes their life as citizens. Unquestionably, therefore, may we assert that the head of the ecclesiastical Hierarchy possesses in an eminent degree the rights which the Hierarchy bestows on its members, and that the Sovereign Pontiff, who is superior to law, should not depend upon secular jurisdiction for competence in matters spiritual or temporal.

---

[290] Conc. Trid., Sess. XXIII *de ref;* c. 6; Sess. XXV *de ref.*, c. 20.

From this fundamental reason flow others. It is not becoming that the supreme legislator should be subject to other laws, except to those which emanate from the Sovereign Pontificate; it is not becoming that he who constitutes the tribunal of appeal for all men, rulers as well as subjects, should be judged by his inferiors. This independence is not comparable to that which can be procured by individual members of the ecclesiastical Hierarchy; but, because of the charge incumbent on him, it is inseparably bound up with the independence of the Church itself, which suffers unjust injury in the perfection of its being and nature when its visible head does not enjoy, with regard to all human power, absolute independence.

The divine law upon which rests pontifical immunity in spiritual things, is also the foundation upon which is built the ecclesiastical law in things partly spiritual and partly temporal. That the Apostolic See is subject to no judgment is affirmed by Boniface VIII in these terms, "The superiority of the Church and ecclesiastical power over the State and civil power is verified by the prophecy of Jeremias, 'I have set thee this day over the nations, and over kingdoms to root up, and to pull down, and to waste, and to destroy, and to build, and to plant.'[281] Therefore, if the earthly power shall go astray, it shall be judged by the spiritual; and if a lessor spiritual power shall go astray, by its superior: but if the supreme power shall go astray, he can be judged by God alone, not by man, according to the Apostle,[282] 'The spiritual man judgeth all things, and he himself is judged of no man.' "[283]

Leo XIII also confirms this traditional view: "The authority of the Supreme Pontificate instituted by Jesus Christ and conferred on St. Peter, and by him on his legitimate successors, the Roman Pontiffs, destined to continue in the world until the consummation of time,

---

[281] Jeremias, I, 10.
[282] I Cor. II. 15.
[283] Bull *Unam Sanctam* in Baronius, *Annales Eccles.* T. XXIII, p. 304.

the propitiatory mission of the Son of God, enriched by the most noble prerogatives, endowed with sublime power, proper and juridical, such as is required in the government of a true and most perfect society, by its very nature and by the express wish of its divine Founder should not only not be subject to any earthly power, but should also enjoy full liberty in the exercise of its high functions.'"[254]

The Roman Pontiff is declared to be free from subjection to any forum or tribunal by the first Canon in *De Fore Competente. "Prima Sedes a nemine judicatur.'*"[255] By the *Prima Sedes* is meant the Roman Pontiff, as is apparent from the nature of the thing.[256] The Sacred Congregations, Tribunals and Offices by means of which the Pope is wont to transact the affairs of the Church are not included in this immunity, and their members may be judged by the Pope himself or by his delegate. The reason why the Pope can be judged by no one is evident. No one can be judged by another unless he is subject to that person, at least with respect to the subject matter of the trial. Now, the Roman Pontiff is the Vicar of Jesus Christ, who is the King of Kings and the Lord of Lords,[257] and to him has been entrusted the commission to feed His lambs and His sheep.[258] In no way, therefore, can he be subjected to any man or to any forum, but is entirely immune from any human judgment. This principle, whether taken juridically or dogmatically suffers no exception.

Beside other texts this is very clearly set forth in Can. 30 of the Council of Rome, and confirmed by the Council of Arles, held in 314 A. D., by Sylvester I, "*Nemo judicabit priman sedem, quoniam omnes sedes a prima sede justitiam desiderant temperari, neque ab Augusto, neque ab omni clero, neque a populo judex judicabitur.*"

---

[254] Letter to Card. Rampolla in *Leonis XIII Acta.* VII, 142.
[255] C. 1556.
[256] Can. 7.
[257] Tim. VI, 15.
[258] John, XXI, 16, 17.

(b) Causes Reserved to the Roman Pontiff.

We may deduce from the above that the Roman Pontiff is the competent judge, even in the first instance, of all persons who belong to the Church, and of all things and causes which look to the forum of the Church. His power is truly a primacy of jurisdiction,[289] which means not only inspection or direction, but legislative, judiciary and executive power throughout the entire Church.

This prerogative embodies a principle acknowledged from time immemorial, viz., the right of appeal to the Holy See from any lower tribunal and at any stage of the trial.[290] The Council of Sardica in 343 clearly outlined this right,[291] and the New Code still vindicates it to the Holy See. Such an appeal, if accepted, suspends the exercise of jurisdiction by the ordinary or delegated judge who has already commenced the trial. Suspension of jurisdiction, however, is not attached to recourse to the Holy See.[292]

Although the Pope enjoys this universal jurisdiction, he reserves to his own exclusive tribunal only certain cases (*causae majores*).[293] These, as given in Can. 1557, para. 1, are:

(1) The cases of actual rulers of nations, their sons or daughters, or the proximate successors of the rulers. Rulers are mentioned generically, not specifically as king, emperor, etc. In a monarchial form of government the ruler is the king or queen, or the person at the head of the government; in a democracy, the presi-

---

[289] Cans. 218-221 embody the Catholic doctrine on the Roman Pontiff. cf. also Pius VI, *Auctorem fidei*, n. 5 (*Denzinger*, ed. 9, 1900, n. 1368); *Decrees of the Vatican Council*, McNabb, p. 42.

[290] Can. 1569, para. 1.

[291] Cf. c. 36, C. 2, q. 6.

[292] Can. 1569, para. 2. The difference between *appeal* and *recourse* is explained in Can. 1889.

[293] Cans. 220, 1600; Leo XIII, Litt. ap., *Trans Oceanum*, Apr. 18, 1897, n. XIV, 3; Conc. Trid. Sess. XXIV *de ref.* c. 5.

dent, or person holding supreme authority. This Canon does not include such persons as Congress, Parliament, Chamber of Deputies, etc., nor their individual members.

(2) The cases, civil as well as criminal, of Cardinals and Legates of the Apostolic See.[294]

(3) The criminal cases of Bishops, titular as well as residential.

Since the middle ages the Pope has been the judge of first instance in all more important episcopal cases (*causae majores, graviores, difficiliores, arduae*), the number and extent of which are in no way exactly definable. Among such cases may be numbered controversies on faith, those concerning the confirmation, translation, deposition, and resignation of Bishops, but above all the more serious criminal charges against Bishops.[295] Causes of major import, whether they are such by reason of their object, e. g., concerning matters of faith; or by reason of the persons, e. g., trial of a Cardinal or a Christian prince, or the disposition of Bishops, are entirely beyond the competence of even the Tribunal of the Sacred Rota.[296] The Roman Pontiff does not generally judge in person, but through delegates who give sentence in his name. He usually allows a hearing of the case by different judges, if it should happen that one of the contending parties, not satisfied with the first sentence, requests this revision from the Sovereign Pontiff himself.

(2) Tribunals Sparing the Labor of the Sovereign Pontiff. The Sacred Congregations are the first bodies to share in the labors of the Sovereign Pontiff, hence Pius X in the Constitution *Sapienti consilio* calls them, together with the Tribunals and Offices, "the Roman Court, dealing with the affairs of the universal Church."

---

[294] Can. 2, X, *de clerico non residente*, III, 4.
[295] Conc. Trid., Sess. XXIV, cap. 5, *de ref.*
[296] Can. 1600; *Lex Propria S. R. Rotae et Signat. Apos.*, Can. 15.

The juridical authority of the Roman Curia is vested in three Tribunals, viz., the Sacred Penitentiary, the Sacred Rota and the Apostolic Signatura. Since the jurisdiction of the Sacred Penitentiary is limited solely to matters which pertain to the internal sacramental and non-sacramental forum, with questions of conscience and decisions regarding the same,[207] it has no place in a treatment of the external forum. Cases requiring judiciary procedure are to be dealt with by the two remaining Tribunals, the Sacred Rota and the Apostolic Signatura, according to the rules laid down in Canons 1598-1605, except the right of the Holy Office and the Sacred Congregation of Rites in cases proper to them.[208]

(a) The Sacred Rota.

There is no more venerable and respected tribunal in the world than the Sacred Roman Rota. In the twelfth and thirteenth centuries, owing to the accumulation of cases for papal jurisdiction, the Popes requisitioned the services of a group of Cardinals and Bishops to assist them in disposing of the cases. The selected Cardinal or Bishop arranged for the suit, heard the evidence of the contending parties, hence the term *Auditor,* and then made his report to the Pope, who gave his decision personally or in a consistory.

The Sacred Rota as a tribunal with definitive jurisdiction dates back to the first decades of the fourteenth century, to the issuance of the famous Constitution *Ratio juris,* by John XXII, in the year 1331. The ordinances therein contained regulated the rights of the Auditors of the Sacred Rota and prescribed the form of oath to be taken by the Auditors and Notaries. Other Popes determined more accurately the constitution and judicial regulations of the Sacred Rota, especially Martin

---

[207] Pius X, Const. *Sapienti consilio,* June 29, 1908, para. II, n. 1.
[208] Can. 259.

V, Constitution *Romani Pontificis providentia,* 1421; Innocent VIII, Constitution *Finem litibus,* 1487; Pius IV, Constitution *In throno justitiae,* 1561; Urban VIII, Briefs *Cum sicut nobis,* 1637, and *Exponi nobis,* 1643.

While in the fourteenth century the number of Auditors appears to have been as many as twenty, it decreased in the fifteenth century to fourteen, and was finally fixed at twelve by Sixtus IV in the Constitution *Romani Pontificis,* 1472, patterned after the numerical quantity of the Apostolic College. The most important matters entrusted to their adjudication were contested benefices and other ecclesiastical civil controversies, and civil cases arising within papal territory.

The power of the Roman Rota was greatest in the fifteenth century. After that, owing to the apostasy of nations during the Reformation, and the gradual acquisition by Roman Congregations of the authority to decide matters which had previously belonged to the competence of the Sacred Rota, its influence was considerably depreciated. When the Roman Pontiff was despoiled of his temporal possessions in 1870, there were no longer any purely civil cases to be tried by this Tribunal and its chief reason for existence was removed. Pius X restored the Sacred Rota, officially establishing its constitution in the Constitution *Sapienti consilio,* June 29, 1908. Moreover, this Tribunal is to be regulated by certain statutes known as the *Lex Propria,* published as an Appendix to the Constitution *Sapienti consilio.* The New Code has affected a few changes in the constitution and competence of the Sacred Rota.[290]

---

[290] Lega, *De Judiciis Ecclesiasticis,* Pars. II, pp. 38-79.
Ojetti, *De Romana Curia,* pp. 175-179.
Martin, *The Roman Curia,* pp. 137-141.
Hilling, *Procedure at the Roman Curia,* pp. 132-137.

(1) Constitution. The Sacred Rota consists of a certain number of prelates,[800] in 1921 they numbered thirteen, all appointed by the Roman Pontiff; they must be priests who have obtained the doctorate, at least in Canon and civil laws,[801] and their head is called the Dean, always the senior Auditor by appointment.[802] The custom is no longer in vogue of reserving three auditor appointments for the City of Rome, two for Spain, one each for Tuscany, Bologna, Ferrara, Venice, Milan, Austria and France. The Sacred Rota judges either in commissions of three Auditors or all together, unless for a particular case the Sovereign Pontiff makes other provisions.[803]

Each Auditor may select an assistant for himself with the approval of the Rotal College and the consent of the Pope; each assistant retains his office at the will of his Auditor.[804] There must also be a Promoter of Justice and a Defender of the bond of marriage, of religious profession and of sacred ordination. These officials must be priests, Doctors of Theology and of Canon Law, appointed by the Pope on the recommendation of the Rotal College.[805] As many Notaries as will be required are to be thus appointed; two of them at least are to be priests who alone are to perform the duties of Notaries in criminal cases of clerics and religious.[806]

(2) Competence. As to the competence of the Sacred Rota, its principal duty in the second instance is to judge of the merit of a cause. The Sacred Rota has jurisdiction in the first instance over (1) residential Bishops in contentious suits, but suits concerning the rights or temporal property of a Bishop, of the epis-

---

[800] Under the *Lex Propria* there were ten prelates, *Lex Propria*. Can. 1, para. 1.

[801] Under the *Lex Propria*, Can. I, para. 2, the doctorate in Theology and Canon Law was required.

[802] Can. 1598, paras. 1, 2, 3.

[803] Can. 1598, para. 4; *Lex Propria*, Can. 11.

[804] *Lex Propria*, Can. 3.

[805] *Id.*, Can. 4.

[806] *Id.*, Can. 5.

copal revenues, or of the diocesan court may with the consent of the Bishop be brought for trial either before the diocesan collegiate tribunal, consisting of the Official and two senior synodal judges,[307] or before the court immediately superior.[308] If the Bishop has not given his consent, the case may not be referred to the diocesan tribunal, but to the judge immediately higher.

(2) The Sacred Rota also judges dioceses and other ecclesiastical moral persons[309] immediately subject to the Roman Pontiff, such as exempt religious organizations and monastic congregations.[310]

Usually a case is first heard in the diocesan court where the Bishop is *ex-officio* the judge. The Sacred Rota also tries in the first instance, besides those cases mentioned in Can. 1557, paras. 2 and 3, the cases, including criminal cases, which the Pope, either *motu proprio*, or at the request of the contesting parties, calls up for his own judgment and commits to the Rota. It decides these cases in the second and third instances, should the need arise and the rescript of commission contain no instructions to the contrary.[311] A new set of three Auditors judges in appeal cases, for example, if a cause is tried by one set and the case is appealed, the set of Auditors immediately following looks to it. If there is need of a third instance, the set immediately following the two preceding sets undertakes the case.[312]

The Sacred Rota is, moreover, the court of appeal for cases already tried judicially in the episcopal tribunals of the first or second instance and legitimately appealed to and accepted by the Holy See. An appeal to be legitimate must not be contrary to Canons 1880 and 666, prohibiting appeal, nor contrary to Canons 1881, 1882, 1886, 1891, laying down the requisites for appeals. Finally, it decides in the last instance, generally the

[307] Those longest in office, Can. 106, para. 3.
[308] Cans. 1557, para. 2, n. 1; 1572, para. 2.
[309] Cans. 99-104.
[310] Can. 1557, para. 2, n. 2.
[311] Can. 1599, para. 2.
[312] Can. 1598, para. 4; *Lex Propria* Can. 14, para. 1.

third, but in cases *de statu personarum,* it may be the fourth, cases, even matrimonial cases, already tried by Rota itself and any other tribunal of second or further instance, as the causes have not become *res judicatae.*[313] By a *res judicata* is meant the controversy in so far as it has been defined by a sentence unassailable by the ordinary remedies of complaint of nullity, or appeal, or the opposition of a third party. Cases *de statu personarum,* e. g., concerning the validity of a marriage, the validity of an ordination, and the validity of a religious profession, never become *res judicatae.*[314]

The competence of the Sacred Rota is sometimes extended to cases brought up in other Congregations. That Congregation or Tribunal or Special Commission which the Pope delegates takes exclusive cognizance of the matrimonial cases of those mentioned in Can. 1557, para. 1, n. 1.[315] Should the Sacred Rota be thus delegated, it would act by delegated power. The Holy Office is competent in matters of faith and morals, and whatever touches the so-called Pauline Privilege, and the impediments of disparity of cult and mixed religion; from which it has power to dispense. All such matters must be referred to that Congregation, which, however, may, if it thinks it opportune and the case permits, refer the question to another Congregation, or to the Tribunal of the S. R. Rota.[316] To the S. Congregation of the Sacraments is referred whatever pertains to the decision and granting of dispensations in matters of marriage and other sacraments. This Congregation is alone competent to decide whether a marriage is consummated, whether the reasons for granting a dispensation truly exist, and all matters connected therewith. However, if it deems it expedient, it may refer any matter to the S. R. Rota.[317] Cases thus referred are judged by the Sacred Rota in the first instance.

---

[313] Can. 1599, para. 1, nn. 1, 2.
[314] Cans. 1903, 1989.
[315] Can. 1962.
[316] Can. 247, para. 3.
[317] Can. 249, para. 3.

There are certain causes which are excluded from the competence of the Sacred Rota. As has been mentioned in the chapter on the Sovereign Pontiff, what are termed *causae majores* are excluded from the competence of this tribunal.[318] Let it suffice to say here that they refer to questions of more than ordinary moment, such as matters of doctrine and the general discipline of the Church,[319] beatification and canonization of saints,[320] the union or dismemberment of dioceses,[321] and those cases reserved to the Roman Pontiff himself in virtue of Can. 1557, para. 1.

There is another class of causes in which the Sacred Rota possess no authority, viz., against decrees of Ordinaries given without observance of judicial procedure there can be no appeal to the Roman Rota nor to any other tribunal; such cases are to be brought before one of the Roman Congregations according to the character of the matter in dispute.[322] These decreees include any extra-judicial dispositions made by the Ordinary, e. g., those mentioned in Canons 2142-2194; penal remedies, Canons 2306-2311; penances, Canons 2312-2313. By *appeal* is meant here judicial application against a judicial sentence, and by *recourse*, extra-judicial application against an administrative decision.

If the Sacred Rota were to examine even incidentally into questions mentioned in the two preceding paragraphs and pronounce sentence, the sentence would be *ipso jure* null.[323]

Under the *Sapienti consilio* the Sacred Rota was competent to deal with petitions to the Holy See to grant

[318] Can. 1600; *Lex Propria,* Can. 15.
[319] Can. 247, paras. 1, 2.
[320] Cans. 253, para. 3; 1999, paras. 1, 2; Lega, *Pars. II,* para. 181.
[321] Const. *Sapienti consilio,* para. I, n. 2, 2; *Normae peculiares,* cap. VII, art. II, nn. 6, 10.
[322] Can. 1601; *Lex Propria,* Can. 16.
[323] Cans. 1558, 1600; *Lex Propria,* Can. 17.

redress in cases in which the law did not recognize the right of appeal for *restitutio in integrum,* in all cases which had passed into a *res judicata* and no remedy could be obtained from the judge of second instance.[334] Now that power is granted to the judge who pronounced the sentence; except in cases where the regulations prescribed by law have been neglected, for then the judge is considered suspected and the tribunal of appeal, which may be the Rota, grants the *restitutio in integrum.*[335] Petitions for restitution to the former judicial status against a Rotal sentence is granted by the Apostolic Signatura.[336]

(b) The Apostolic Signatura.

When the Rota was first established and a number of papal chaplains were thereby separated from the immediate judiciary offices of the Pope, those remaining continued to inform the Pope in judicial matters. To them was given the name *Referendarii* or Apostolic Referees. Their particular task was to examine the matter under consideration, decide whether it should be brought to the notice of the ecclesiastical tribunals, and also which court would be competent. Their chief duty, therefore, was to judge of the form of a cause. The Pope thus reserved to himself supreme jurisdiction.

The term *Signatura* originated from the custom of the Sovereign Pontiff, when various kinds of petitions were sent to him, to affix to the answer of each petition his signature. Consequently the office that prepared the petitions for his signature became known as the *Signatura.*

For a long time the Referees worked out separate opinions on submitted communications. With the

---

[334] *Lex Propria,* Can. 14, para. 4.
[335] Can. 1906.
[336] Can. 1603, para. 4.

increasing number of petitions, Alexander VI divided the Referees into two bodies, the *Signatura justitiae,* to edit decrees concerning judicial affairs, and the *Signatura gratiae,* to deal with questions of favors. One was established to execute acts of justice; the other, acts of clemency.

Sixtus V reduced to one hundred the number of Referees of the *Signatura justitiae;* and to seventy, those constituting the *Signatura gratiae.* He also eliminated many unnecessary qualifications required in prospective Referees.[327] Alexander VII,[328] from the Referees of both Signaturae formed a college of twelve, who possessed the power of voting, *Prelati votanti;* those remaining *Referendarii simplices,* were devoid of this power. Leo XII[329] bestowed on the Referees the title of nobility. Finally Gregory XVI[330] organized the *Signatura justitiae,* bestowing on it competence to decide: (1) petitions to suspend or to declare invalid proceedings and findings of courts; (2) disputes about competency among judges and courts; (3) controversies concerning the consolidation and recalling of causes; (4) questions concerning objections against judges because of legitimate suspicions; (5) petitions for granting a new appeal. He took little notice of the *Signatura gratiae,* which had gradually fallen into desuetude. The last Cardinal-Prefect of this Signatura died in 1839, and from the year 1847 we find no mention made of it in catalogs of the Tribunals and Officials of the Roman Curia.[331]

In dealing with the restoration of the Apostolic Signatura, the Constitution *Sapienti consilio* limits its remarks to these words, "We have also deemed it well to restore the supreme Tribunal of the Apostolic Signa-

---

[327] Const. *Quemadmodum,* Sept. 22, 1586.
[328] Const. *Inter ceteras,* June 13, 1659.
[329] *Motu proprio, Quum plurima,* April 15, 1826.
[330] *Motu proprio, Elevati appena,* Nov. 10, 1834.
[331] Ojetti, *De Romana Curia,* pp. 187-194; Lega, *De Judiciis Ecclesiasticis, loc. cit.,* pp. 27-37.

tura and by these present letters we do restore it, or rather we institute it in the manner determined in the above-mentioned law (*Lex Propria*), suppressing the ancient organization of the Tribunals of the Papal Signatura of Grace and of Justice.'"[332]

(1) Constitution. This tribunal consists of a number of Cardinals chosen by the Sovereign Pontiff, who also designates one of them as Prefect.[333] The Roman Pontiff likewise appoints an Assistant or Secretary, who under the direction of the Prefect and in accordance with the regulations of the Apostolic Signatura is to do all that may be required in the preparation and expedition of cases.[334] There are also appointed at least one Notary to take charge of the archives and to assist the Secretary, and one custodian of the office chamber of the Signatura. The former official should be a priest; the latter, a layman.[335] A number of Consultors are appointed by the Sovereign Pontiff to examine whatever questions are to be presented to the tribunal for a vote. Whatever regulations have been made for the Officials of the Sacred Rota in regard to their nomination, oath of office, obligation to observe secrecy, and general discipline are to be observed proportionately by the officers of this Tribunal.[336]

(2) Competence. The present Signatura exercises ordinary jurisdiction in the following cases:

(a) In accusations brought against one or more of the Auditors of the Sacred Rota on the ground of violation of secrecy, or on the ground of damages inflicted through null or unjust acts in their judicial capacity.[337]

---

[332] Const. *Sapienti consilio*, para. II, n. 3.

[333] Under the *Lex Propria*, Tit. II, Can. 35, para. 1, they numbered six; the New Code, Can. 1602, leaves the number indefinite. In 1921 there were seven Cardinals on this Tribunal.

[334] *Lex Propria*, Can. 35, para. 2.

[335] *Loc cit.*, Can. 36.

[336] *Loc. cit.*, Can. 36, paras. 2, 3.

[337] Can. 1603, para. 1, n. 1; *Lex Propria*, Cans. 9, 37, n. 2.

The Auditors of the Rota are always bound to observe inviolable secrecy regarding the discussion held in the collegiate tribunal before sentence was passed, including also the various votes and opinions therein expressed.[338]

Should they dare to violate this secret or communicate to others in any way the secret acts[339] they may be punished by fines and other punishments, not excluding the loss of their office, according to the gravity of the accusation, or even severer, if particular statutes provide severer penalties.[340] The nullity of their action would arise from a judicial fault, e. g., by declaring without good reason that they were competent; its injustice, for example, from refusing to administer justice when they were certainly and evidently competent to do so. If the violation of the secret or the inflicted injuries occurred in a criminal case, and an appeal be made, the Signatura is the Tribunal from which to obtain it.[341]

(b) In accusations of suspicion brought against an Auditor of the Rota.[342] Some causes of such suspicion are consanguinity or affinity in any degree in the direct line and in the first and second degrees in the collateral line; guardianship and direction, intimate association, intense hatred, the desire of financial compensation or of avoiding injury, or previous connection with the case in the capacity of advocate or procurator.[343] In a case of suspicion the Apostolic Signatura is to determine whether or not the suspicion is true; that done, it sends back its decision to the Rota, which proceeds according to its ordinary rules, the Auditor against whom the exception was taken remaining in or being excluded from his proper place.[344]

---

[338] Can. 1623, para. 2.
[339] Mentioned in Can. 1623, para. 3.
[340] Can. 1625, para. 2.
[341] Can. 1604, para. 1.
[342] Can. 1603, para. 1, n. 2.
[343] Can. 1613, para. 1.
[344] Can. 1604, para. 2.

(c) Complaints of nullity against a Rotal sentence.[345] Complaints of nullity may be distinguished into those made separate from appeals and those united with appeals. Complaints of nullity made separate from appeals are heard by the judge who passed the null sentence. This Canon (1603, para. 3) constitutes an exception to that rule in behalf of the Sacred Rota. What if the complaint of nullity be added to an appeal? Such a cause, Noval[346] likens it to a connected cause,[347] would fall under the competence of the judge of appeal, in this case the Rotal set of Auditors before whom the appeal together with the complaint was brought. The Signatura is to judge only whether the Rotal sentence was null, and then return the case to the Rota, unless his Holiness makes other provisions.[348]

(d) Petitions for *restitutio in integrum* against a decision of the Rota that has already become *res judicata.*[349] It is not necessary that both conformable decisions required for a *res judicata* be given by the Sacred Rota; if the last of two conformable decisions be given by it, that suffices. The Signatura judges only as to whether *restitutio in integrum* is to be conceded or not,[350] in accordance with Can. 1905. Restitution against the sentences of other tribunals is governed by Can. 1906.

Competence of the Signatura in the four above-mentioned cases is found in Can. 37 of the *Lex Propria.* The next two cases of competence are an amplification granted by Benedict XIV in his Constitution *Attentis expositis,* June 28, 1915, and embodied in the New Code.

(e) Recourses against Rotal decisions in matrimonial cases which the Rota has refused to submit to a new examination.[351] Recourses are dealt with here, not

[345] Can. 1603, para. 1, n. 3.
[346] *De Processibus,* Pars. 1, p. 105.
[347] Can. 1567.
[348] Can 1604, para. 3.
[349] Can. 1603, para. 1, n. 4.
[350] Can. 1604, para. 3.
[351] Can. 1603, para. 1, n. 5.

appeals. For example, if the Sacred Rota gave the second sentence (C. 1987) concerning the validity of a marriage, and no appeal was made within the legitimate time (Cans. 1881, 1986), should the parties desire to avail themselves of the law that sentences in matrimonial cases never pass into a *res judicata* (C. 1989) recourse must be made to the Apostolic Signatura. The Signatura decides whether the recourse is to be admitted or not, and then returns the case to the Rota.[352]

The concluding phrase of Can. 1604, para. 3—"*nisi Sanctissimus aliter providerit*" is liable to be misinterpreted. Noval, *De Processibus,* Para. 1, p. 107, commenting on it, says, "whence it is inferred that the judgment of the Signatura Apostolic in cases of nullity, *restitutio in integrum* or recourse is not definitive unless subjected to the cosideration and approbation of the Holy Father." This interpretation is contrary to Can. 244, para. 2, "All favors and explanations need pontifical approbation, except the sentences of the Sacred Rota and the Signatura Apostolic." It would seem that the phrase refers rather to the nature of the decision of the Signatura, viz., that the Signatura is to judge only *de forma causae,* unless the Pope otherwise provides for it to judge also *de merito causae.*

(f) The conflict in competence which may arise between inferior tribunals is settled as follows:[353] if the controversy on competence arises between two Bishops or suffragan Officials of the same Archbishop, the Metropolitan court settles it. If the controversy arises between two Bishops or suffragan Officials of different Metropolitans, the dispute is settled by the Metropolitan of the judge before whom the action was first brought. If the controversy is between two judges immediately subject to the Holy See, e. g., two Metropolitans or Prelates

---

[352] Can. 1604, para. 3.
[353] Can. 1603, para. 1, n. 6.

nullius, if there is an Apostolic Delegate, he decides the question; if there is no Apostolic Delegate, the Apostolic Signatura renders the decision.[354]

If a controversy about competence should arise between the Sacred Congregations, Tribunals or Offices of the Roman Curia, it is settled by an assembly of Cardinals whom the Roman Pontiff shall designate for each case.[355] This is an entirely new enactment. Formerly the Consistorial Congregation had power to settle all such controversies about competence, which were quite numerous after the *Sapienti consilio* first went into effect.

The Signatura has delegated power in petitions sent to his Holiness *per supplices libellos* to obtain the commission of a cause to the Sacred Rota.[356]

A *libellus* is a declaration of an intended action made in writing. The *libellus* in this connection contains extra-judicial petitions to have tried by the Rota a case which does not belong *ex se* to the Rota (*i. e.* according to Can. 1599, paras. 1 & 2) and which has not been committed to it by a *motu proprio* of the Pope (Can. 1599, para. 2, *aliasve . . . . . . succedunt*).

In the examination of these petitions, the Signatura, when it has the proper knowledge and has heard those concerned, determines whether or not the petitions are to be granted.[357]

Very probably, although judging with only delegated power, the Signatura need not submit its decision for the approval of the Sovereign Pontiff.

The sentences of the Supreme Tribunal of the Signatura are valid even though the reasons *in facto et in jure* are not therein contained.[358] Decisions of all the other Tribunals, even the Sacred Rota, must under pain of

---

[354] Can. 1612.
[355] Can. 245.
[356] Can. 1603, para. 2.
[357] Can. 1604, para. 4.
[358] Can. 1605, para. 1; Can. 1873, para. 1, n. 3.

nullity contain the reasons or motives for imposing sentence.[559] Nevertheless, either at the urgent request of one of the parties or *ex officio*, if the case demands it, the Supreme Tribunal can make known its reasons, in accordance with its own proper regulations.[560] The general regulations are (1) those of the common law (C. 1555, para. 2) and (2) those laid down in *Lex Propria* (C. 43) and not contrary to the common law. The specific regulations will be found in the New Code, Can. 1907, and in the *Lex Propria*, Cans. 38, 40.

---

[559] Can. 1873, para. 1, n. 3; Can. 1894, n. 2; *Lex Propria*, Can. 32, para. 3; *Regulae serv.*, Append. III, para. 182.

[560] Can. 1605, para. 2.

BIBLIOGRAPHY

SOURCES.

Acta Apostolicae Sedis, Romae, 1909-1922.

Acta et Decreta Concilii Plenarii Baltimorensis II, Baltimorae, 1868.

Acta et Decreta Concilii Plenarii Baltimorensis III, Baltimorae, 1886.

Acta Sanctae Sedis, Romae, 1865-1908.

Analecta Ecclesiastica, Romae, 1893, sqq.

Analecta Juris Pontificii, Romae, 1855-1890.

Canones et Decreta Sacr. Concilii Tridentini, Romae, 1904.

Canonical Legislation Concerning Religious, Authorized English Translation, Rome, 1918.

Code, Juris Canonici, Pii X, Pontificis Maximi, Jussu Digestus, Benedicti Papae XV Auctoritate Promulgatus, Romae, 1917.

Collectanea Sacrae Congregationis de Propaganda Fide, 2 Vol., Romae, 1907.

Corpus Juris Canonici, Editio Lipsiensis, Richter-Friedberg, 2 Vol., Lipsiae, 1879-1881.

Leonis XIII, Pontificis Maximi, Acta, vol. VII, *Romae,* 1888.

Mansi, *Sacrorum Conciliorum Nova et Amplissima Collectio,* Parisiis, 1901-1913.

AUTHORS.

Aichner, *Compendium Juris Ecclesiastici,* ed. IX, Brixinae, 1900.

American Ecclesiastical Review, *The New Canon Law in its Practical Aspects,* Phila., 1918.

Amos, *History and Principles of the Civil Law of Rome,* London, 1883.

Augustine, *A Commentary on Canon Law,* 7 vols., St. Louis, 1918-1921.

Baart, *The Roman Court,* Milwaukee, 1895.

Baart, *Legal Formulary,* New York, 1898.

Bargilliat, *Praelectiones Juris Canonici,* 2 vol., Parisiis, 1915.

Baronius, *Annales Ecclesiastici,* tom. XXIII, Parisiis, 1871.

Bassibey, *Le Mariage devant les Tribuneaux Ecclesiastiques,—Procedure Matrimoniale Generale,* Paris, 1899.

Benedictus XIV, *Opera Omnia,* 17 vol., Prati, 1839-1847.

Blackstone—Cooley, *Commentaries on the Laws of England,* 4th ed., Chicago, 1899.

Blat, *Commentarium Textus Codicis Juris Canonici, Liber II: De Personis,* Romae, 1919.

Boudinhon, *Le Mariage Religieux et le Proces en Nullite,* Paris, 1900.

Bouix, *Tractatus De Judiciis Ecclesiasticis,* 2 vol., Parisiis, 1883.

Bouix, *Tractatus De Principiis Juris Canonici,* Parisiis, 1882.

Brandi, *I Cardinali di S. R. Chiesa nel Diritto Publico Italiano,* Roma, 1905.

Canoniste Contemporain, 1878 sqq.

Cappello, *Institutiones Juris Publici Ecclesiastici,* 2 vol., Romae, 1907.

Cappello, *De Censuris juxta Codicem Juris Canonici,* Taurinorum Augustae, 1919.

Cappello, *De Curia Romana,* Romae, 1913.

Catholic Encyclopedia, 15 vols., New York, 1917.

Catholic Encyclopedia, *Supplement on Canon Law,* New York, 1917.

Cavagnis, *Institutiones Juris Publici Ecclesiastici,* 3 vol., Romae, 1882.

Clark, *History of Roman Private Law,* 4 vols., Cambridge, 1906-1919.

Cocchi, *Commentarium in Codicem Juris Canonici, Liber I: Normae Generales,* Taurinorum Augustae, 1920.

Cocchi, *Commentarium in Codicem Juris Canonici, Liber II: De Personis, P. I.,* Taurinorum Augustae, 1922.

D'Annibale, *Summula Theologiae Moralis,* Romae, 1896.

De Smet, *De Sponsalibus et de Matrimonio,* ed. III, 2 vol., Bruges, 1920.

Demeuran, *L'Eglise, Constitution—Droit Public,* Paris, 1914.

Denzinger, *Enchiridion Symbolorum et Definitionum,* Friburgi in Br., 1908.

Edwards, *Ecclesiastical Jurisdiction,* London, 1853.

Encyclopedia Americana, Art. *Canon Law,* vol. V, New York, 1920.

Encyclopedia Brittanica, Art. *Domicile,* vol. VIII, New York, 1910.

Esmein, *Le Mariage en Droit Canonique,* Paris, 1891.

Evans, *Obligations,* Philadelphia, 1826.

Fagnanus, *Jus Canonicum, sive Commentaria Absolutissima in Quinque Libros Decretalium,* Venetiis, 1764.

Fanfani, *De Jure Religiosorum ad Normam Codicis Juris Canonici,* Taurinorum Augustae, 1920.

Ferraris, *Prompta Bibliotheca,* Romae, 1899.

Ferreres, *Institutiones Canonicae,* 2 vol., Barcinonae, 1917.

Fourneret, *Le Domicile Matrimonial,* Paris, 1906.

Fourneret, *La Reforme de la Curie Romaine,* in Le Canoniste Contemporaine, vol. 33, pp. 16, 65.

Fulton, *Index Canonum,* New York, 1883.

Gasparolo, *Jus Civile Romanum,* vol. V, Senis, 1904.

Gasparri, Henricus, *De Domicilio et Quasi-Domicilio,* Romae, 1897.

Gasparri, Pietro Card., *Tractatus Canonicus De Matrimonio,* 2 vol., Paris, 1904.

Girard, *Histoire de L'Organization Judiciare des Romains,* Paris, 1901.

Hilling, *Procedure at the Roman Curia,* New York, 1907.

Lega, *De Judiciis Ecclesiasticis,* 4 vol., Romae, 1896-1901.

Lombardi, *Juris Canonici Privati Institutiones,* 3 vol., Romae, 1901.

McNabb, *The Decrees of the Vatican Council,* London, 1907.

Mansella, *De Impedimentis Matrimonialibus ac de Processu Judiciali,* Romae, 1881.

Martin, *The Roman Curia,* New York, 1913.

Menochius, *De Immunitate Ecclesiastica,* Genevae, 1695.

Menochius, *De Jurisdictione Ecclesiastica et Saeculari,* Genevae, 1695.

Mommsen, *Le Droit Public Romain,* 7 vol., Paris, 1891.

Monin, *De Curia Romana,* Lovanii, 1912.

Moyle, *Institutes of Justinian,* 4th ed., Oxford, 1906.

Noval, *Commentarium Codicis Juris Canonici, Liber IV: De Processibus, Pars I, De Judiciis,* Romae, 1920.

Noval, *Codificationis Juris Canonici Notitia Generalis,* Romae, 1918.

Nussi, *Conventiones inter Sanctam Sedem et Civilem Potestatem,* Romae, 1870.

O'Donnell, *Domicile: Historical Development of the Idea,* Irish Theological Quarterly, vol. X, 129.

O'Donnell, *Domicile: Canon Law at Present* (1916), Irish Theol. Quar., vol. XI, 294.

O'Donnell, *Quasi-Domicile: Historical Development of the Idea,* Irish Theological Quarterly, vol. XI, 26.

O'Donnell, *Quasi-Domicile: Canon Law at Present* (1917), Irish Theol. Quar., vol. XII, 230.

Ojetti, *Synopsis Rerum Moralium et Juris Pontificii*, ed. 3, 4 vol., Romae, 1909-1914.

Ojetti, *De Romana Curia*, Romae, 1910.

Parsons, *Studies in Church History*, 6 vols., New York, 1901.

Peries, *Code de la Procedure Canonique dans les Causes Matrimoniales*, Paris, 1894.

Peries, *La Procedure Canonique Moderne dans les Causes Disciplinaires et Criminelles*, Paris, 1898.

Pierantonelli, *Praxis Fori Ecclesiastici*, Romae, 1883.

Pighi, *Censurae Sententiae Latae Quas Habet Codex Juris Canonici cum Brevi Commentario*, Veronae, 1917.

Pihring, *Jus Canonicum in Quinque Libros Decretalium Distributum*, Venetiis, 1759.

Pitra, *Juris Ecclesiastici Graecorum Historia et Monumenta*, 2 vol., Romae, 1864.

Prichard-Nasmith, *History of Roman Law*, London, 1871.

Pycia, *Momentum Juris Civilis Romani*, Kielciis, 1907.

Ravail, *De L'Object de la Possession: Essai sur le Droit Romain*, Paris, 1899.

Raviart, *Traite des Actions Possessoires*, Paris, 1904.

Reiffenstuel, *Jus Canonicum Universum*, tom. II, Venetiis, 1735.

Resemans, *De Competentia Civili in Vinculum Conjugale Infidelium*, Romae, 1887.

Ricci, *Praxis Rerum Quotidianarum Ecclesiastici Fori*, Venetiis, 1674.

Sanchez, *Disputationum de Sancto Matrimonii Sacramento Libri Tres*, Antwerpiae, 1620.

Schaff-Wace, *Nicene and Post-Nicene Fathers, Second Series*, New York, 1905.

Schmalzgrueber, *Jus Ecclesiasticum Universum,* 6 vol., Romae, 1843-1845.

Smith, *Elements of Ecclesiastical Law,* 2 vols., New York, 1887-1888.

Smith, *The New Procedure in Criminal and Disciplinary Causes of Ecclesiastics in the United States,* New York, 1888.

Sohm, *Institutes of Roman Law,* 4th Eng. ed., Oxford, 1892.

Strachan-Davidson, *Problems of the Roman Criminal Law,* 2 vols., Oxford, 1912.

Thomassin, *Ancienne et Nouvelle Discipline de L'Eglise,* Bar-le-Duc, 1864.

Trezzini, *La Legislazione Canonica di Papa S. Gelasio* I, Locarno, 1911.

Van Espen, *Opera Omnia Canonica,* 2 vol., Venetiis, 1769.

Wernz, *Jus Decretalium,* ed. 3, 9 vol., Romae, 1913-1915.

Wynne, *The Great Encyclical Letters of Leo XIII,* New York, 1903.

Zitelli, *Apparatus Juris Ecclesiastici,* Ratisbonae, 1903.

Universitas Catholica Americae

Washingtonii, D. C.

Sacra Facultas Theologica

1921-1922

No. 14

CANONES

DEUS LUX MEA

CANONES

QUOS

AD DOCTORATUS GRADUM

IN

JURE CANONICO

Apud Universitatem Catholicam Americae

CONSEQUENDUM

PUBLICE PROPUGNABIT

THOMAS JOSEPHUS BURKE

SACERDOS ARCHIDIOECESIS PHILADELPHIENSIS

JURIS CANONICI LICENTIATUS

HORA X. A. M., DIE XXVII. MAII A. D. MCMXXII

XXVI.	Canones	1043-1044	De Ordinariorum et Sacerdotum Potestate Dispensandi, Urgente Mortis Periculo.
XXVII.	Canones	1060-1064	De Impedimento Mixtae Religionis.
XXVIII.	Canon	1068	De Impedimento Impotentiae.
XXIX.	Canones	1133-1137	De Convalidatione Simplici.
XXX.	Canones	1138-1141	De Sanatione in Radice.
XXXI.	Canones	1552-1553	De Judiciorum Ecclesiasticorum Notione, Objecto, et Divisione Ratione Objecti.
XXXII.	Canones	1554, 1933	De Causis Mixti Fori.
XXXIII.	Canones	1556-1558, 1569	De Foro Romani Pontificis.
XXXIV.	Canon	1559	De Foro Adeundo ab Actore.
XXXV.	Canon	1560	De Foro Competenti Necessario.
XXXVI.	Canones	1561-1568	De Foris Voluntariis.
XXXVII.	Canones	1572-1579	De Judice Primae Instantiae.
XXXVIII.	Canones	1594-1596	De Tribunali Secundae Instantiae.
XXXIX.	Canon	1598	De Constitutione Sacrae Romanae Rotae.
XL.	Canones	1599-1601	De Competentia Sacrae Romanae Rotae.
XLI.	Canon	1602	De Constitutione Signaturae Apostolicae.
XLII.	Canones	1603-1605	De Competentia Signaturae Apostolicae.
XLIII.	Canones	1636-1639	De Loco et Tempore Judicii.
XLIV.	Canones	1679-1683	De Actionibus ob Nullitatem Actorum.
XLV.	Canones	1690-1692	De Mutuis Petitionibus.

XLVI.	Canones	1825-1828	De Presumptionibus.
XLVII.	Canones	1960-1965	De Foro Competenti in Causis Matrimonialibus.
XLVIII.	Canones	1986-1989	De Appelationibus in Causis Matrimonialibus.
XLIX.	Canones	1990-1992	De Processu Administrativo in Causis Matrimonialibus.
L.	Canones	1993-1998	De Causis Contra Sacram Ordinationem.
LI.	Canones	2186-2194	De Suspensione ex Informata Conscientia.
LII.	Canones	2195-2198	De Natura Delicti Ejusque Divisione.
LIII.	Canones	2215-2219	De Poenarum Notione, Speciebus, Interpretatione atque Applicatione.
LIV.	Canones	2236-2240	De Poenarum Remissione.
LV.	Canones	2241-2244	De Natura Censurarum.
LVI.	Canones	2245-2247	De Reservatione Censurarum.
LVII.	Canones	2248-2254	De Absolutione Censurarum.
LVIII.	Canones	2306-2311	De Remediis Poenalibus.
LIX.	Canones	2368, 904	De Poenis in Solicitantes.
LX.	Canones	2369, 889-890	De Poenis in Violantes Sigillum Sacrementale.

Vidit Sacra Facultas:

CAROLUS F. AIKEN, S. T. D., p. t. Decanus

H. SCHUMACHER, S. T. D., p. t. a Secretis.

Vidit Rector Universitatis:

†THOMAS J. SHAHAN, S. T. D., J. U. L., LL. D.

LIFE.

Thomas Joseph Burke was born in Philadelphia, Penna., November 23, 1894. He received his elementary education in the public and the parochial schools and his secondary training in the Roman Catholic High School of that city. On September 9, 1912, he entered St. Charles Seminary, Overbrook, Pa., and was ordained to the priesthood May 29, 1920. The following September he entered the Catholic University of America, Washington, D. C., and attended the lectures of the Rt. Rev. Msgr. Filippo Bernardini, S. T. D., J. U. D., in Canon Law, of the Rev. Peter Guilday, Ph. D., in American Church History, of the Rev. Bernard A. McKenna, S. T. D., in Mariology. On June 15, 1921, he received the degrees of S. T. B., J. C. B., J. C. L.

He is happy to have this occasion to express to his professors and instructors his sincere gratitude and appreciation for the kindly interest manifested in his studies. In particular, he wishes to acknowledge his indebtedness to Msgr. Bernardini, under whose direction this monograph was written; to the Very Rev. Charles F. Aiken, S. T. D., and the Very Rev. Daniel J. Kennedy, O. P., S. T. M., for their careful revision of the manuscript in preparing it for the press.

www.ingramcontent.com/pod-product-compliance
Lightning Source LLC
LaVergne TN
LVHW050202080826
844660LV00012B/338

9780813222059